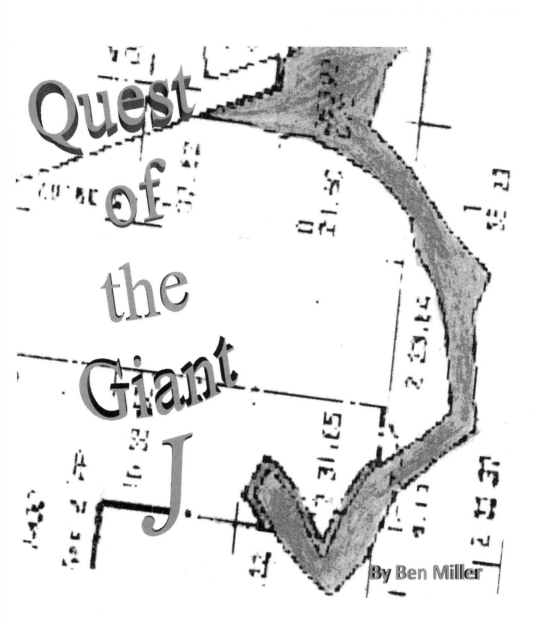

Quest of the Giant J.

By Ben Miller

Table of Contents

<u>*Quest of the Giant J*</u>

The Most Interesting Giant J Goldmine In The World Reveals To A Man Who Is A Cousin of General Andrew Jackson, General Stonewall Jackson, & A 4th Great Grandson of Jesse Woodson James:

The Legendary Jesse James, Secrets Of The Knights Templar & Confederate Treasures, & The Lost Gold Mines Of The American West

By Ben Miller

<u>*Chapter 1*</u>
<u>*The Quest Begins*</u>

Ben was working as a Sales Engineer representing some of the largest CNC machine

builders in the world while in his spare time pursuing his hobby interests of music and archeology.

He graduated with honors from Northern Illinois University in Dec 2001 with a Bachelors of

Science degree in Business Management along with an emphasis in Technology and Archeology.

After graduation in his spare time Ben began recording songs that he had written on guitar over the

years and released 2 full albums between 2003 and 2005. His career was going well in the machine

tool industry as a Sales Engineer and he had surpassed his million dollar quota in sales.

Just before thanksgiving in 2005 Ben received a call from the Senior VP of Warner Bros Music who had given him great reviews on his second album and discussed the potential for a record deal.

Ben was encouraged to keep playing and make another album which he began compiling after work in

2006.

It was also around this time that he began researching potential treasure stories and archeology sites

near his home in the suburbs of Chicago. Ben had already done extensive research into his Native

American heritage which was inspired by an event that took place when he was a young boy.

Ben was being pushed back and forth in a circle of 3rd graders when he was in 2nd grade and

was being called names and being used as a human football. His eyes started to tear. As tears started to

come to the surface he looked up at the kids in the circle and to his amazement Ben saw another circle

of old Indians that had surrounded the older 3rd grade kids although they could not see the Indians.

Ben's eyes connected with one old Indian in particular and the Indian spoke to Ben through

telepathy without actually speaking. He said, "You are one of us and you better start acting like it."

The next thing Ben knew was that his body was moving up and down and his legs started dancing. He

was doing a dance that he had never been taught before. Energy came over his whole body as if he

were plugged into an electrical outlet. The older kids immediately recognized this as a Native

American attribute and the smallest of the older kids said holy crap it's a wild Indian. Ben then turned and punched the tallest kid in the face and then turned and punched the smallest kid. The others started

to run as Ben turned towards them with absolutely no more fear . Ben was more worried about

disappointing the old Indians that nobody could see because he recognized their

power as something obviously very powerful. After that day the 3rd grade never picked on the second

graders again and Ben would remember that day for the rest of his life. It was really the old Indians

that had left the impression in his mind that maybe he was related to them since they said he was one of

them. In fact, Ben did eventually learn that he was part Native American when he was a bit older and

was eventually told on his 21st birthday by his grandmother on his father's side that he was Apache.

By the time Ben finally found out what tribe he was related to he had already done extensive research

on native cultures of all kinds and was fascinated by the history and cultures of such brave people. He

had also recently verified a relation to 2 Indian Chiefs and one of them being the famous "Chief

Victorio" aka "Apache Wolf" of the Chiricahua Apache.

This whole experience of understanding who he was inevitably guided Ben in the future with

the notion that you should care about your ancestors and who they were because even though you may

not have ever met them they care for you and watch out for you and can even help you like they did

that day on the playground.

Ben was told by his other grandmother on his mother's side that they were related to Andrew

Jackson and she had been told by her grandmother. Of course his reaction out of shock was "you mean Andrew Jackson the President? the guy on the 20 dollar bill? The Army General of Tennessee?"

Yes, that is the same Andrew Jackson that she was talking about and he would certainly find out the truth soon enough with the help of his Apache tracking capabilities which seemed to be somewhat hereditary for some reason. Ben was pretty good at investigating and tracking things for some reason and he knew it was one of his natural abilities.

When he was a young boy occasionally his grandma would mention that her grandpa Jack had lots of land somewhere and that he was a big hillbilly from Tennessee.

As a young boy the term hillbilly carried a somewhat negative feeling along with it for some reason. It would be many years later that Ben would learn the true meaning and origination of the name which seemed to completely change the once negative image in his mind.

The term hillbilly originated in northern Ireland and was used to describe the groups of Scots-Irish settlers that had settled in the hills of northern Ireland. Ben was looking at family pictures and documents that his grandmother had received from her grandpa Jack. It appeared the land that had been mentioned by his grandma in the past actually had some photos associated with it. Ben studied these photos intensely and certainly recognized that these were old photos and from another time when life was maybe less complex in some ways but also more difficult in many other ways.

Ben wondered what his great-great grandfather could teach him about life and survival from an 1890's

or early 1900's perspective which is around the time the photos were taken.

Ben's grandma wasn't sure where exactly the property was located but the log home picture had

the Black Hills written on the back and she knew that was her grandpa Jackson's goldmine property

where her mother was raised until age 5.

It appeared there was also a few people in the fort picture that were wearing civil war hats or

military hats of some kind but Ben's grandmother was not aware if her grandpa Jackson was in the

military or not but she was positive that he owned the gold mining business that he was involved with in South Dakota and that it was his biggest venture but she also mentioned that he was involved with many businesses over the years and was also involved in building the first movie theater on Chicago's North Side after the gold mining days.

Ben was confused as to why his grandma didn't really seem all that interested in this black and white photo of a gold mine operation. She apparently thought it was her grandfathers old saw mill operation and didn't realize this larger saw mill photo was actually the gold mining operation and a military fortification for the famous Jackson Brigade headquarters . Her grandpa Jackson had also turned the business in the Black Hills into a sawmill operation as well. She didn't realize that the large building photo was actually the gold mining operation before the sawmill had been added yet. Ben's grandmother was told she was related to General Andrew Jackson but she always thought of it as a joke for some reason. Ben was beginning to see very quickly how easy it is for family information to be lost over time or forgotten like an old watch that gets put in a drawer for years or decades.

Ben's grandma made the promise that if he could find the property and if their was anything of

value left she would grant him the entire Jackson estate which she rightfully inherited from her

grandparents in the 1950's. Ben had read an article about private properties sometimes called "Federal

Enclaves" located in federal jurisdiction that were immune to state taxation. Sometimes military officers were compensated with land as payment for services rendered. Congress didn't intend for these

pioneers to pay property taxes for county resources they would never use while settling the wild west

on desolate mountains in a national forests virtually far from any resources that the county provided.

These people settling these federal mineral patents were in the middle of nowhere for the most part and

often within range of hostile Indian country. Ben thought that if he was related to General Andrew

Jackson then it is possible that his great great grandpa Jackson acquired property in federal jurisdiction

and was possibly also in the military.

His grandma wasn't sure if he was military or not she said but he played the fiddle and owned a

lot of businesses on the north side of Chicago after the Gold Rush days. The bottom line is that this

mining property is probably located on a mountain somewhere and Ben's grandmother has never had the need or desire to visit. Her mother was conceived and raised on the property but she herself had

never been there so there was a sense of generational detachment that Ben had to comprehend before

learning more.

She is telling Ben that no other male in the family has been to her grandfathers gold mine in the Black

Hills since he shut the operation down in the 1900's. Ben felt pretty confident for some reason that if

he could only find this place there was a chance that this property was a "federal enclave" in federal

jurisdiction. He also felt like it would be pretty cool to see the spot where his 2nd great grandpa had

built his cabin in the middle of nowhere on a mountain.

Ben started to think about survival and how he thought his grandpa Jack who appeared to be a

tall slender hillbilly from Tennessee seemed to know a lot about surviving off the land in a very

mountainous terrain. There were mountains visible in both the cabin and fort/gold mill picture.

Ben thought this whole situation was strange but immediately thought the odds of being related to

Andrew Jackson were looking pretty possible after all just based on the size of this fort.

He wasn't positive that it was even a fort yet but he was pretty positive that at least 2 people in the

photo were wearing civil war hats or officer hats and his grandpa Jackson was wearing a Tennessee or

Missouri type disc hat that was similar to what Jesse James was reported to wear.

Ben noticed his grandpa Jackson looked like a big hillbilly from Tennessee and actually had some very similar facial features like the nose that was a prominent Irish trait that was prevalent in much of the Jackson side of Ben's family. Ben's great great grandpa Jackson and his grandma both had the exact same nose features as Andrew Jackson. Then he compared photos of General Stonewall Jackson who had claimed to be 2nd cousins to Andrew Jackson but historians have had difficulty linking them in the family tree. Ben could see that Stonewall had the exact same long Nordic nose facial features as well.

He thought well that is strange but it could just be a Scotch-Irish thing since he knew for sure that Andrew Jackson was at least Scotch Irish just like his grandpa Jackson.

Ben set out to find this property that had been lost in the family photos and history since the 1950's. So how do you find a piece of property when you have to search 100 square miles of the Black Hills as your perimeter?

First of all the fort photo says Tennessee on the back but he can tell that it's most likely in the Black Hills just like the cabin which also has mountains in the background and his grandpa Jack is wearing the same outfit in both pictures. Ben thought the women in his family were amateur investigators at best so why be surprised. Ben's college degree has a minor in Archeology so he already had a natural interest in history and investigating the past civilizations. This was going to be a great little investigative challenge as an Archaeologist Ben thought to himself and also as a Genealogist if he can prove that he is related to Andrew Jackson like his grandma was told, that would be a very cool thing to verify as well.

In 2007 Ben ordered several land entry files from the National Archives to verify the owners of the mineral and land patents issued to the Jackson surname. He ordered the original entry files for every patent issued to John or Jack Jackson in the Black Hills region. The actual land patents themselves can be ordered separately for $1.50 ea from the BLM but they generally only have the owners name and location of the property.

With a name like John/Jack Jackson this could prove to be more difficult than originally thought. Ben checked about 14 files and did not find his grandparents listed in any of them.

Well where the hell is this land then he said to himself. It then occurred to him that since the fort/mill building in the old photo was so huge the patent could have been issued under his grandfathers business name. It also occurred to him that the Dakota Territory originally included Montana and North Dakota as well.

Then he thought what if it's not in South Dakota at all. This really was turning out to be a challenge. If he can't find the property their will be no way to determine the ownership of the Jackson estate. Ben asked his grandma if she knew the name of her grandfathers company but she could not remember anything other than it was his biggest business ventures including building

the first Nickelodeon movie theater on Chicago's North Side. Ben ordered more land patents and

continued the search. He ordered every patent of relevance to his grandpa Jackson's name located in

the original Dakota Territory adding a huge stack of paperwork to his desk in his already clustered

home office. Ben checked them all and again came up empty. None of the federal census info for the

Black Hills had his family on it either after doing a thorough check. That just didn't make any sense he

thought. He looked at the picture of the fort which he had blown up to a 4 foot poster for his office

wall above the bulletin board. He would shout at the picture and say "Jack , where are you? If pictures

could talk he bet this one would be able to possibly.

None of the patents were a match. It had to be under the business name and that was going to be very

difficult to find out without the location. Ben was starting to lose his patience with this treasure hunt

not to mention the small fortune in patent and archive fees was now over $200.

Ben started to think the whole thing is bullshit. He couldn't find anything in the history books about a

Colonel Jackson after the Lt General Stonewall was killed in the civil war in 1863. He thought about

giving up the search and putting all this stuff back in the drawer for a rainy day. Ben had been

searching for this property in his free time for almost 2 years now. It certainly wasn't his job but in many ways was starting to feel like a part time job. Ben couldn't drop the issue. It was nagging at him

every day. He couldn't stand the thought of failing as an archeologist and not being able to track down

the location of his family property.

He started to realize that it was his responsibility because his grandma had three daughters who

never would have been interested in this old mining business anyway.

Ben caught a second wind and realized that he had what it takes to get something like this done

when most people would have given up after 2 weeks or 2 months. Ben was still going strong after 2

years of intense research.

He had accumulated a massive wealth of info on the history of land acquisition in the United

States. He had studied the military tactics used by Army Colonels and various Generals engaged in

Guerrilla warfare throughout hostile Indian country. He learned that the fierce Apache skills and

masterful tactics of guerrilla warfare were first recorded in the field by army officers and then retaught

to potential Generals at West Point Military Academy out of a 400 page manifesto.

Ben being part Apache himself has always held an interest related to anything Native American. The

American western frontier was a wild and unforgiving place that had little or no rules until the creation

of territories which were put under the command of a Federal Territorial Colonel.

Ben started to talk with other archeologists in the region that maybe had a better knowledge of the history of the Dakota Territory. He figured back to square one. We have to use the picture he

thought.

No one will recognize the cabin photo but the fort is a huge building. Someone has to know

where this was located.

The photo has got to be connected to a land or mineral patent of some kind.

As part of the method by which the new United States decided to dispose of its territories, it created in

the Constitution an article, section, and clause, that specifically dealt with such disposals. Article IV,

Section III, Clause II, states in part, "The Congress shall have Power to dispose of and make all needful

Rules and Regulations respecting the Territory or other Property belonging to the United States." Thus,

Congress was given the power to create a vehicle to divest the Federal Government of all its right and

interest in the land. This vehicle, known as the land patent, was to forever divest the federal

government of its land and was to place such total ownership in the hands of the sovereign freeholders

who collectively created the government. The land patents issued prior to the initial date of recognition of the United States Constitution were ratified by the members of Constitutional

Congress. Those patents created by statute after March, 1789, had only the power of the statutes and

the Congressional intent behind such statutes as a reference and basis for the determination of their

powers and operational effect originally and in the American system of land ownership today.

As has been seen, man is always striving to protect his rights, the most dear being the absolute right to

ownership of the land, This right was guaranteed by the land patent, the public policy of the Congress,

and the legislative intent behind the Statutes at Large. Such rights must be reacquired through the

redeclaration of the patent in the color of title claimant's name, based on his color of title and

possession. With such reborn rights, the land is protected from the forced sale because of delinquency

on a promissory note and foreclosure on the mortgage. This protected land will not eliminate the debt, a

trust must be created whereby "partners" will work together to repay it. These rights must be recaptured

from the state legislated laws, or the freedoms guaranteed in the Bill of Rights and Constitution will be

lost. Once lost, those rights will be exceedingly hard to reclaim, and quite possibly, as Thomas

Jefferson said, the children of this generation may someday wake up homeless on the land their

forefathers founded. On a different note, Ben had also been given a badge and gun that was framed by his grandma and had been in the family for many years but the story behind it was not quite clear.

The badge and gun was in the home office of a 2nd cousin to Ben's great grandmother and belonged to her husband who was a Retired Chicago Police Sergeant. Years ago Ben had made a few calls to try and determine who the badge was issued to but did not have any luck. On the back of the frame there was a description that said the badge and gun were issued to Marshall Ketchpaw or Kitchpao.

Ben's grandma had kept the gun in the family even after selling all the other guns that her late husband had collected over the years. She knew this gun had been used by a family member but the story had faded over many decades years.

It appeared to be a native American name and even though Ben had done extensive research on American Indian tribes during his Archeology studies he could not find any matches to any native American surnames in any tribe. Some people on Ancestry.com said it was German.

A Chicago Police historical website said that personnel files were

written on index cards somewhere in the human resources department which were not kept anywhere externally and might require an extensive search. Ben put the badge and revolver research on hold for a later time or until more information could be discovered but it has been on his list of things to do for

about 10 years now.

He did extensive research into the name Ketchpaw and found absolutely nothing

and was starting to think that the info would be impossible to find without physically going down to the

police headquarters and searching by hand himself which would have to wait until later as usual.

"Stonewall and Old Hickory" : 150 Year Bloodline Mystery Solved
Chapter 2

Ben made calls to several northern district archeologists who seemed willing to talk about the

situation and some offered their ideas on how to find the lost building. They all seemed to think the

picture looked like the Black Hills though so that was a positive. It was at this time that Ben mentioned

to his friends that he was feeling better about the situation because he was talking with other

archeologists who showed some encouragement for the project but his friends and his wife were both

starting to think Ben was becoming obsessive and would probably never find the property.

In fact several people said that he would never find it with just an old picture.

Ben wasn't giving up though for some reason, he just felt he had to do this and that his ancestors

would guide him in his search. Plus, he was the archeologist he told himself and the doubters will eventually be proven wrong if he could only find this property before his hair turns gray.

Ben would imagine himself inside the cabin by himself reading a book or tending to the fire just like his grandpa Jack would have done on a cool evening.

Ben was reading books about the lost Confederate treasures buried by the Knights of the Golden Circle (KGC) for when the south would rise again. These books also covered a lot about Freemasons and the Knights Templar and how their rituals and secrets had influenced the KGC. The KGC was essentially a secret cabinet of the Confederate Army that was considered easily the most powerful spy network to ever operate within the borders of the United States.

Ben always knew that his grandmas grandfathers family was from Tennessee but he himself was from Chicago and that is where his grandpa Jackson had retired and died as well.

Ben's great great grandpa Jackson was born in White Bluff, Tennessee in 1866 and that is where the search begins for trying to find the link to General Andrew Jackson.

Ben had a feeling that if he could only locate the property in this black and white photo from 1900 that he would possibly find more information as to who his grandpa Jackson really was after all and why he appears to have his own military fortification in the Black Hills.

Ben began reading and researching Andrew Jackson and the various secret societies that he was associated with like the Freemasons and perhaps the Knights Templar.

Ben would have to wait up to 3 months for many of the land documents to arrive from the National Archives so he used this time to try and learn more about his family history.

The census records for the Jackson family in White Bluff, TN. were relatively easy to find once Ben realized that his grandpa Jackson's middle initial was different on the 1870 census than on the 1880 census which had caused some confusion.

The Dickson County archives had some information for Ben from a book that had been written by a cousin who had already done previous research on the Jackson family from White Bluff.

Jack's father's name was George Washington Jackson and his mother was Rebecca Jackson and he had at least a few brothers and a couple sisters. According to the census records the family had owned over 4000 acres prior to and after the civil war which had ended in 1865 the year before Great Great-Grandpa Jackson was born in 1866.

George Washington Jackson was born in 1829 and was the son of Peter Jackson born in 1800.

Peter Jackson was the son of Willis Jackson born in 1770 in Virginia.

According to the family research done by his distant cousin in Tennessee Peter Jackson had donated the land for the old school house in White Bluff which is still there today.

Ben had gotten the phone number for his lost cousin Tony Hammond from the Dickson county archives who had written the book on the Jackson history. Ben was pretty shocked after talking with

Tony who apparently had always been told by elders that his Jackson line was 1st cousins to General

Stonewall Jackson and was also 2nd cousins to President Andrew Jackson but the connection to

Andrew

1880 United States Federal Census

Name:	**G. W. Jackson**
Home in 1880:	District 12, Dickson, Tennessee
Age:	51
Estimated Birth Year:	abt 1829
Birthplace:	Tennessee
Relation to Head of Household:	Self (Head)
Spouse's Name:	Rebecca Jackson
Father's birthplace:	Tennessee
Mother's birthplace:	Tennessee
Neighbors:	
Occupation:	Farmer
Marital Status:	Married
Race:	White
Gender:	Male
Cannot read/write:	
Blind:	
Deaf and dumb:	
Otherwise disabled:	
Idiotic or insane:	

Household Members	Name	Age
	G. W. Jackson	51
	Rebecca Jackson	46
	Bennie Jackson	24
	George Jackson	22
	Mary E. Jackson	18
	Ella Jackson	16
	Jackson J. Jackson	14
	Mittie A. Jackson	12
	Wm. Overton Jackson	8

had never been verified mainly because researchers had failed to connect Stonewall and Andrew

together through their paternal line. Tony was a direct descendant from Benjamin Franklin Jackson the

brother of George Washington Jackson Ben's 3rd great grandfather.

Ben's grandma was told she was related to President Andrew Jackson but now

General Stonewall Jackson was a new addition to the mystery.

Now Ben had another General to consider with his search trying to link his family to General Andrew

Jackson.

Ben started to receive more papers from the archives in the following months. None of them

were a match to his information once again.

He researched all known forts in the Dakota's as well but came up with nothing once again. Ben

was really becoming frustrated and his best of friends were starting to see his frustration as a sign of

failure but Ben wouldn't let go.

During the day Ben sells machinery that is used in machine shops and fabrication houses in

the industrial sector all across Northern Illinois. He decided to start his own business

and had acquired a few product lines from his father and grandfather who were also well established

Sales Engineers in the area with their own businesses.

Ben caught a break one afternoon while sitting in his home office working on the Jackson

genealogy project. In between making sales calls he would slip in a call to historians or archaeologists

in the Dakotas and continue searching for his family's property. An archaeologist from the Northern

US District called him back and said that he was confident that he could find the building after looking

at the picture of the fort. He said said no one will know where this cabin is located but this building is

huge and someone must have documented it. He assured Ben that it was definitely in the Black Hills

from looking at the pictures and that he needed a little time to check his resources. About a week went

by and then Ben got a call from Jay Newman the District Archaeologist in South Dakota and Jay

said he had found the fort.

Not only did he find it but he had found another picture of it in a book about railroads in the

Black Hills.

It was recorded as the Mystic Mill in 1904 in "Railroads of the Black Hills" by Mildred

Fielder and the photo was originally in "Black Hills Illustrated".

Ben's search had finally come to an end.

Amazingly, Ben and Jay the Archaeologists had finally found the location of the fort only by using the

picture that everyone said would never work.

Well actually Ben wasn't there yet. The book had very little info about the business or its exact

location but by this time Ben had become a Topographical map expert and had already marked a place

on the map called the Lookout Mill near the town of Mystic which was on an old map from the 1890's.

On the map it was called the Lookout Mill because it was in the Lookout mining district. With the old topographical map Ben was able to search the patents by township,section, and range for all the patents in that section. He was very happy to see that there were only 2 patents issued in that area of the Lookout Mining District. Ben called up the National Archives and ordered the patents directly instead of sending the forms through the mail. He ordered the patents original entry files as well which should have more info about his grandpa Jackson's business and those involved.

He also ordered the plat map of the patent from the Bureau of Land Management(BLM) in Montana which also handles the patent records for the Dakotas except the original entry files which are kept at the National Archives in Washington DC.

Ben had ordered so many patents that he had become quite familiar with the laws and language that were written in them. He started to find patents issued to other family members that were definitely related that had also settled land out west. Some were mineral and some were just regular land patents usually acquired under the Homestead act or paid for in cash outright.

He had noticed that there were land patents and mineral patents on both sides of his family. Some were one page long and some were several pages long. It appeared that the mineral patents had several pages of survey info and the regular land patents are just one page long generally.

The mineral patents have conditions and stipulations of sale that appear to be federal laws and written for the benefit of the owner.

Ben felt like he had a huge weight lifted from his shoulders when finally ordering that last patent. On and off for a little over 2 years in his spare time he searched for this piece of paper that would be coming in the mail any day now.

He knew it would be a mineral patent based on his search narrowing it down to two potential mineral patents and two company's that operated in that section and township.

Meanwhile, Ben was diving deeper into his own family history and studying the history and ways of the Masons and the Knights Templar. Andrew Jackson was a documented 33rd degree master mason.

Ben wondered if "Old Hickory" General Andrew Jackson was somehow his grandfather or a cousin. How does General Stonewall Jackson fit into the picture? These were 2 of the greatest General's in the history of the United States according to most military experts and war historians.

Andrew's orders to build a moat in the battle of New Orleans War of 1812 was pure genius and heavily aided the underdog and outnumbered Tennessee militia against the same advancing British army that defeated the famous and ruthless French commander Napoleon. If General Andrew Jackson and the

Tennessee militia didn't stop that invasion the USA would be part of the United Kingdom right now because they had already destroyed the north and were trying to close the gap from the south through Orleans.

The Tennessee militia completely annihilated the invasion of over 7000 British with General Andrew Jackson sending Choctaw, Cherokee, and Chickasaw raiding parties at night time which infuriated the British General who sent a letter of disgust but Andrews response was that from the moment they set foot on American soil all hell would be unleashed and they would not be allowed to rest.

After receiving info from the Dickson County Archives in Tennessee Ben began working on the genealogy again and sure enough was able to find the link to Stonewall Jackson and President Andrew Jackson almost immediately believe it or not. Ben plugged in his new Jackson family information from Tennessee into his family tree that was growing quickly.

He had already started a family tree on the Miller side which had gone all the way back to his 4th great grandfather Calisto Olguin who was listed as a Spaniard that settled near a a Native American community of Socorro,Texas but was born in Socorro, New Mexico in 1792.

Ben had discovered that he was also most likely related to a famous Apache Chief as well or at the very least from the same band of Eastern Chiricahua Apache as Victorio aka "Apache Wolf".

Anyone can see that this genealogy can get very confusing the farther you go back especially when trying to connect cousins. It was as if Ben's new Jackson information was not only a key to his family history but also linked to the country's history.

This particular Jackson line had been researched by over 70 other people on Ancestry.com and have linked the name all the way back to Yorkshire, England in 1290. Ben thought this is wild. How could this be documented so well? He looked at the information intently and it was certainly all aligning correctly and noted that the confusion was always about who the father really was for Andrew Jackson Sr. who had died before the General was born in 1767. Historians have debated that it was either Hugh Jackson or Dr Joseph Jackson and Ben's family line clearly was showing that Andrews Grandfather was Joseph Jackson and that his parents were John Jackson and Katherine McKinley who were immigrants from Ireland and also the documented Great Great Grandparents of Lt General Stonewall Jackson.

Ben had unraveled a mystery that historians have been debating for 150 years. Mystery solved he thought but he had a feeling things were just starting to be revealed.

So Stonewalls Great Grandfather Capt John Jackson born in 1715 was an immigrant from Ireland and was the son of John Jackson born in 1667 Ireland and he was the son of Anthony Jackson

II born in 1599. Anthony Jackson II was the grandson of Anthony Jackson born in 1535 who is also the 12th great grandfather in Ben's Jackson line.

Andrew's grandfather Dr. Joseph Jackson was brothers to Stonewalls Great grandfather Capt John Jackson. Andrew's father Andrew Jackson Sr. was 1st cousins to Stonewalls grandfather Colonel Edward Jackson and 1st cousins removed to Stonewalls father John Jackson and 2nd cousins to Stonewall himself.

It appears that General Stonewall was telling the truth when he said that he was 2nd cousins to General Andrew Jackson. Amazing Ben thought, this mystery had baffled historians for so long and he had the answer hidden in his family tree all along. Amazing he exclaimed!

Other historians have documented the Jackson family in the UK very well actually do to their political involvement in Scotland and Ireland. Historians have pointed out that Anthony II was the son of Sir Richard I who was Knighted by King James in the 1500's during an invasion of England.

Ben's grandma was told that she was related to Andrew Jackson and Ben had proven that myth to be true. Ben was able to verify that he was cousins to both Stonewall and Old Hickory and that they all have the exact same paternal line and the same great grandfather in Medieval Knight Sir Richard Jackson from the 1500's. Based on Ancestry.com's simulated family tree it appears that Stonewall and Andrew are 6th and 7th cousins to Ben that are 6 and

7 times removed. It was really their common great grandfathers that were 1st cousins dating back to the

1600's.

Ben was shocked at the moment as he was beginning to see the potential connection to the

Knights Templar which was certainly no more than a movie fantasy less than 10 minutes ago it

seemed.

The Templar's were banned from France in the 1300's mainly due to the fact that the King Philip of

France had owed them a large amount of money and was becoming threatened by their political

power and vast amounts of wealth which included massive land holdings they had acquired.

The Templar's were a military order originally called the Poor Knights of Christ and officially

endorsed by the Catholic church in 1129 AD.

They were organized to protect peaceful travelers from Muslim attacks traveling between old

Europe and the holy land. They had reportedly acquired the Ark of The Covenant and a massive

treasure from King Solomon's Temple although no one has ever been able to verify any of that to be

fact. Two other rumors are that they acquired a document called the "San Greal" or Holy Grail from

the Temple as well. Another spelling or interpretation of the document is spelled slightly differently

"Sang Real" meaning Royal Blood.

Ben was thoroughly delighted that he had solved a historical mystery but was also amazed to

find that his direct relation to Stonewall and Andrew Jackson had led him straight into another mystery

regarding knighthood. What does it mean to be knighted by a king? Were the rest of his grandfathers

after the 1500's knights as well. How do the Knights of the Golden Circle relate to the knights of King

James and the UK if at all?

It was summer time in 2007 when Ben had been designated as the sole heir and owner of the

Jackson Estate which took almost 2 years to find due to the fact that federal mineral

patents didn't really have an address. These properties were in the middle of nowhere usually on top of

mountains in the middle of desolate national forest areas.

It was a a sunny afternoon in late July when Ben checked his mail box and found an envelope

from the National Archives in Washington DC. He opened the envelope and looked at the documents

which was a huge stack of entry files for the 2 company's that had received mineral patents in the

section that he had located the Lookout Mill. Ben's eyes lit up

as he was starring at an appraisal from the Bureau of Land Management for the building that he had a

picture of from the late 1890's.

This was the correct mineral patent and in the entry files the building had been described as the

Blossom Mill. The company was the Blossom Gold Mining Company and the patent was issued in 1895. The topographical maps from the 1890's had the building marked as a landmark called the Lookout Mill. The railroad book had called it the Mystic Mill and another report from a civil war Confederate veteran's diary had referred to it as Fort Lookout. So all together there were 4 different names associated with the building in various documented sources. Ben didn't really care what it was called he was just very happy to have finally found his family's property. The first building on the appraisal after the Fort was the log home that Ben also had a picture of and all the dimensions matched for both buildings exactly.

Ben had recognized the name Merritt H. Day that was on the board of Directors of his family business who was none other than the Territory Colonel of all of Western South Dakota. Ben immediately ordered as much documented historical information that he could find regarding the Colonels activities and sure enough it became clear that this was a military operation.

The State Archive records along with personal diary information from soldiers that served under his command had described how many soldiers from civil war had served in the Indians wars out west almost immediately after the civil war had officially ended in 1865.

The most recognized military arm of the Confederate army was the Stonewall Jackson Brigade that had won more battles than any other Brigade in the civil war under the command of Lt General

Stonewall Jackson. Ben then realized that when his cousin Lt. General Stonewall was killed in battle it

was considered a huge blow to the Confederate forces and it was then that his Jackson line had been

put in charge of the Stonewall Jackson Brigade immediately after Stonewalls death.

Ben was once again in shock and the movie National Treasure Book of Secrets immediately

came to mind regarding the KGC and the Confederates acquiring Cibola the lost city of gold in the

Black Hills of South Dakota. The movie asserted that if the (KGC) Knights of the Golden Circle

acquired Cibola then the south would have won the Civil War for sure and that was apparently their

goal. What Ben was looking at was a potential connection to the Confederate's that actually verified

this small bit of information that was previously thought to be completely fictional.

It's a ridiculous concept to even think the south won the civil war he thought. Most people

would laugh at that comment especially since Americans in general were taught in public schools

nationwide that the north won the war.

Ben thought about President Abraham Lincoln and how he was assassinated after the war had already

ended apparently which the movie also had referenced KGC involvement in that as well.

Ben had read that the KGC supposedly went underground after the civil war and was active in the

United States until 1916 when they sealed their records for the next 50 years until after the last remaining member was dead. Ben read parts of the Holt report that was a military report compiled by the union army during the civil war regarding the KGC activities and the serious nature of the organization's powerful military spy structure. The KGC was certainly real and they certainly were known to exist during the civil war. What most people don't know is that they existed after the civil war. Ben was struggling with the fact that the war obviously didn't end when everybody thinks it did and that the KGC was still running around carrying out covert operations. Lincoln's assassination was carried out by John Wilkes Booth who was a member of the White Camellia's which was associated with the KGC. So if Lincoln was killed by the KGC or its associates and the civil war was officially over what else did the the KGC do exactly and when did the civil war really end in reality.

Ben wondered how a supposedly fictional movie could be so accurate when determining where Cibola was located because at this point Ben had already verified through research that if there ever was a Cibola it was most likely in the Black Hills because the largest gold mine in the world was only 20 miles from his family's property.

This whole situation seemed very ironic. Ben began wondering who was the KGC really and

why does it appear that his family who were Confederate veterans from the Stonewall Brigade were

potentially also connected to this mysterious secret cabinet of the Confederate Army called the Knights

of the Golden Circle(KGC).

Well actually it does make sense because Stonewall was a Lt General and second in command

to General Lee of the entire Confederate Army. So it would make sense that if their were a secret

cabinet of some kind that Stonewall would probably know about it which means his cousins would

possibly also know about it.

There are a lot of questions that remain but at this point after years of searching and trying to

find his families mining property Ben had finally accomplished the task and felt pretty fantastic

overall. Now that he found the location he could order the plat map and file his inheritance of the

mineral patent with the county.

In college, Ben's Bachelor of Science degree had an Emphasis in Archeology so his love for history and archeology in this whole adventure was certainly adding to his desire to investigate more.

After all it was his own family's history and he felt an obligation to his grandma and to his ancestors

not to mention it was extremely interesting.

Chapter 3
The Journey West

Ben bought all the necessary supplies and survival gadgets that one could think of that he didn't already own. This was after all going to be an adventure into the wilderness and to a very desolate location. He ordered the plat map and it took just a few days to arrive from the BLM. He opened the map and was starring intently at the map when he just started laughing out loud as his dogs looked on in confusion. It's amazing! Inconceivable! Unbelievable! Extraordinary! The property was in the shape of a letter J. A Giant J actually!

Ben's great great grandpa Colonel Jackson C. Jackson had settled a piece of mining

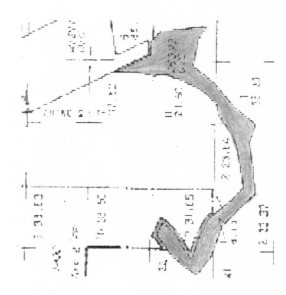

property in the shape of a 72 acre giant J.

If you flip the oddly shaped J it becomes a C.

Ben thought it obviously stands for JC Jackson but possibly could not help thinking about its possible

reference to Cibola as well.

Ben wondered if his grandma was playing a trick on him. How could she not know that the place her

mother was raised was a gold mine in the shape of a giant J? Inconceivable. Well, apparently

according to experts the KGC kept the women in the dark for their own protection. The women were

probably never even aware that they were living on a giant J carved out of the wilderness by the

Colonel and his brigade.

Ben showed his grandma the map of the giant J and her whole face lit up the

room in joy. She was obviously unaware of the situation. By now it was pretty apparent that Ben had

stumbled on to something significant. His grandma was not really sure of the value of the estate but it

always seemed so far away from Chicago that she would probably never even see it let alone rent an

excavator and start digging for gold but Ben gave it some serious consideration. His grandma said she

hopes he finds gold nuggets the size of his fist and reassured him that her grandpa Jackson would be

very proud of his efforts.

Ben was immediately arranging a trip and preparing the Jackson estate documents that were

signed by his grandma and the public notary.

He booked his first vacation to the Black Hills for November 5th 2007 with his friend Chuck Vargas.

Ben and Chuck were old high school buddies and Chuck had agreed to go along for a small 4 day

break.

They said goodbye to their wives and left at 9pm and drove through the night listening to Coast to

Coast Am on the radio.

The nest day they checked into the hotel and ventured out to see the Crazy Horse monument
and Mt.

Rushmore at night after getting something to eat at a local Diner.

The hills were amazing and the locals in town seemed very nice as well.

The mission was to obtain photos of the property and ascertain the current status of any remaining

buildings such as the Log Home or the Fort/Mill.

They took a road that connected to a gravel road that took them into the mining district and the

scenery was breath taking.

There was a huge black wild mustang down the road from the fort sitting in

a field.

The mountains and trees were amazing and picturesque in every way. Deer

and wild turkeys were seen running off as Ben drove his 4x4 Jeep through the mountain terrain.

Chuck Vargas was holding the GPS as they approached the destination point. After winding through

some rough

turns in between a creek and a mountain they were finally approaching the property.

It was vast and had huge mountains on all sides with a creek running through the entire giant J

property.

Chuck looked at Ben and said I think this property is a money maker. They stopped at the Fort

which was still there but in a giant pile of debris. Chuck had pointed out that the Mill had been forced

to the ground with a bulldozer but the steel re-bar and massive beams were to large to remove.

Ben had learned from some locals that the building was destroyed relatively recently.

A gold miner/mountain man named Jim stopped by in an old pick up truck and said to look for

rocks with a yellow tint to them because there's a good chance it's gold. He also mentioned that the

owner Jack had given him the authority to be the care taker of the property. Ben had a discussion about

the fact that he was the mineral rights owner but realized that there was obviously somebody else claiming some type of ownership to something. He figured he would finish his vacation and figure that

out later.

Ben and Chuck checked out the mine which had been sealed off with fencing

and someone had placed no trespassing signs in the area.

Ben thought the signs looked kind of new but figured the forest service had done this for safety

reasons.

They drove around the mountain and found the log home location along with scattered debris that were

positively identifiable as being from grandpa Jack's cabin but that was pretty much it. They found the

chimney flashing and the actual bed that was likely used in the cabin. Ben thought that his blood line

could have been created on this bed so they took pictures and documented the find. They spent the last

two days searching for gold. They found an actual wild bull wandering around in the pasture just past

the giant J property which seemed almost like a spirit that was starring back at them.

At the end of the day during the last hour of hunting Ben said out loud to

the spirit of his great great grandpa Jack in a rather frustrated tone "Jack where is the damn gold". Ben

picked up a few more rocks which he put in his pocket and then they left as the sun was beginning to

go down.

Back at the hotel Ben was checking his rock finds and sure enough one of the last rocks he put in his pocket appeared to contain gold.

Once back in Chicago Ben had the rock tested for gold at 3 different places and sure enough it passed the 22.5 carat nitric acid test. Back at the home office Ben was reading through the massive stack of mineral entry papers from the National Archives and he discovered that the mine was called the "Black Eagle" and was 7500 ft long. The mining operation consisted of removing a vein of gold that was accessed from the giant J property but went deep into the hills surrounding the perimeter. They used elevated rail carts to carry the removed material down to the mill where the rocks were crushed up by the 40 stamp mill and then the gold was sifted out through a series of sluice boxes designed to filter out the smaller finer gold particles. It appeared that the state and local historical authorities had no information on the operation or the huge fort/mill in the middle of the Black Hills.

Ben was amazed at the amount of gold involved and wondered where it all was located today. The mineral patent had mentioned something about a vein outcropping but Ben had no idea that it went that deep and so much had been removed.

Ben went back to the Black Hills in 2009 for another vacation with another friend and was unable to spend much time on the property. In fact almost immediately after he and his friend Carl Hobie had gotten out of the jeep they were informed that they were trespassing and that the owner had called the Sheriff. Ben was curious as to what was going on so they waited for the half hour before the Sheriff showed up.

In the meantime Ben was searching for gold in the same spot that he had found gold the last time he was there. He said the same thing out loud so Carl could hear as if it were a signal to the spirit world "Jack where is the damn gold". He paused for a second after and looked around the area with a gaze of an eagle and his eye caught "the sight of a glimmer in a sea of dullness". He walked over and picked up a pretty large rock about baseball size. It appeared to have gold shining through so he put the rock in his pocket.

The Sheriff pulled up shortly after and said they were trespassing and had to leave. Ben was informed that the county had sold his family's property in a tax sale and the guy who called the police was the current tax owner on file. Ben informed them that the property was federal jurisdiction and that there were no property taxes on his federal mineral premises or his federal right to dig for his minerals.

The Sheriff said the District Attorney says that a judge will have to authorize our ownership.

Ben was very upset but left his family's mountain home in the hands of a stranger at the demand of a

county Sheriff that appeared to be trespassing in federal jurisdiction.

Back at the hotel Ben was examining the large rock he had picked up. It was pretty heavy maybe 3

pounds but he could not tell if it were mostly gold or not. There was certainly gold though for sure he

told himself. Carl and Ben headed to the Diner for some dinner and Ben brought the rock with him

because he figured it might be worth more than the his Jeep if it was solid gold. He could not risk a

hotel cleaning person stumbling across the golden rock in the room. He took several photos with his

phone and sent them to his father. Ben was confident that he had found gold but it was still a mystery

until they could get the rock tested. The next day Ben and Carl reluctantly left and headed the 13 hours

back to Chicago. The weather was beautiful in late August 2009 as they blazed across the plains

talking about the situation that had suddenly become intense. Ben was also pretty sure that the big rock

he picked up really did have gold in it but Carl was skeptical because they really were only out of the

car for 30-40 minutes tops and Carl didn't see anything but rocks. On the way back Ben tried not to let

the Sheriff experience ruin the whole trip but it was difficult to think about anything else. Ben just

described the situation as looking into a vast sea of dullness and seeing a glimmer of shiny gold in the

distance as if his eyesight had somehow changed while on the property.

It was as if Ben had acquired tunnel vision and was able to see a rock among thousands that had

contained gold even from 20 feet away. Ben could not really explain it himself other than he had a

very strong spiritual connection with his ancestors and the giant J property.

The Litigators
Chapter 4

Ben got back to the home office and unleashed a fury of phone calls and filed a complaint with

the Department of Justice. He began reading as much about mineral rights as he could find and

contacting numerous attorneys and land people. One attorney told him to read about his rights and sent

him an article to read.

Bitter disputes over valuable natural resources such as those depicted in old Hollywood

Westerns are thought by many landowners to be an obsolete artifact of the past and a relic of the

lawless frontier. But thanks to an increasingly sophisticated legal system, the potential for controversy

regarding the interpretation of mineral rights is even greater now than it was in the American Wild

West.

Ben knew that knowing the ins and outs of mineral rights is crucial for any new landowner.

The key to a successful and lucrative transaction involving mineral assets is expert assistance from

those who understand real estate, geology, market value, and the legal nuances that specifically apply to

mineral rights agreements. Because minerals in the ground are not readily visible to the naked eye they may seem mysterious and intangible. But the process of protecting or transferring mineral rights is not

necessarily exotic if one has experienced legal counsel. Minerals in the ground can be conveyed like

any other type of property and bought, sold, leased, or optioned. Buying or selling a home or tract of

land without problems typically requires help from professionals including Realtors, attorneys,

inspectors, and appraisers. Likewise, those who get help from qualified experts in the area of mineral

rights law can avoid all the pitfalls associated with mineral leases while reaping the full financial

benefits.

, the said placer mining premises hereinbefore described;

TO HAVE AND TO HOLD said mining premises, together with all the rights, privileges, immunities, and appurtenances of whatsoever nature thereunto belonging, unto the said grantee   above named and to   **her heirs**
and assigns forever; subject nevertheless to the following conditions and stipulations:

FIRST. That the grant hereby made is restricted in its exterior limits to the boundaries of the said mining premises, and to any veins or lodes of quartz or other rock in place bearing gold, silver, cinnabar, lead, tin, copper, or other valuable deposits, which may have been discovered within said limits subsequent to and which were not known to exist on   **March 17, 1910.**

SECOND. That should any vein or lode of quartz or other rock in place bearing gold, silver, cinnabar, lead, tin, copper, or other valuable deposits, be claimed or known to exist within the above-described premises at said last-named date, the same is expressly excepted and excluded from these presents.

THIRD. That the premises hereby conveyed shall be held subject to any vested and accrued water rights for mining, agricultural, manufacturing, or other purposes, and rights to ditches and reservoirs used in connection with such water rights as may be recognized and acknowledged by the local laws, customs, and decisions of the courts. And there is reserved from the lands hereby granted a right of way thereon for ditches or canals constructed by the authority of the United States.

FOURTH. That in the absence of necessary legislation by Congress, the Legislature of   **Colorado**
may provide rules for working the mining claim or premises hereby granted, involving easements, drainage, and other necessary means to the complete development thereof

IN TESTIMONY WHEREOF, I,   **Woodrow Wilson**

President of the United States of America, have caused these letters to be made Patent, and the Seal of the General Land Office to be hereunto affixed.

GIVEN under my hand, at the City of Washington, the   **THIRTIETH**

(SEAL)   day of   **JUNE**   in the year of our Lord one thousand

nine hundred and   **THIRTEEN**   and of the Independence of the

United States the one hundred and   **THIRTY-SEVENTH.**

By the President: *Woodrow Wilson*

This is a mineral patent containing federal conditions and stipulations of sale with stipulation # 4 delegating Legislative authority to Congress making the premises federal jurisdiction essentially. The county governments have illegally taxed these premises and trespassed in federal jurisdiction leading to massive property destruction and theft thru fraud and corruption.

The United States of America,

To all to whom these presents shall come, Greeting:

Homestead Certificate No. 13176.

Application 24399.

WHEREAS, There has been deposited in the GENERAL LAND OFFICE of the United States a Certificate of the Register of the Land Office at Devils Lake, North Dakota, whereby it appears that, pursuant to the Act of Congress approved 20th May, 1862, "To secure Homesteads to Actual Settlers on the Public Domain," and the acts supplemental thereto, the claim of

NILS E. AHLGREN

has been established and duly consummated, in conformity to law, for the Lot four of Section twenty and the north half of the southeast quarter and the Lots one and two of Section seventeen in Township one hundred fifty-seven north of Range seventy-one west of the Fifth Principal Meridian, North Dakota, containing one hundred sixty-two acres,

according to the Official Plat of the Survey of the said Land, returned to the GENERAL LAND OFFICE by the Surveyor General:

NOW KNOW YE, That there is, therefore, granted by the UNITED STATES unto the said

Nils E. Ahlgren

the tract of Land above described; TO HAVE AND TO HOLD the said tract of Land, with the appurtenances thereof, unto the said Nils E. Ahlgren

and to his heirs and assigns forever; subject to any vested and accrued water rights for mining, agricultural, manufacturing, or other purposes, and rights to ditches and reservoirs used in connection with such water rights, as may be recognized and acknowledged by the local customs, laws, and decisions of courts, and also subject to the right of the proprietor of a vein or lode to extract and remove his ore therefrom, should the same be found to penetrate or intersect the premises hereby granted, as provided by law.

IN TESTIMONY WHEREOF, I, Theodore Roosevelt , President of the United States of America, have caused these letters to be made Patent, and the seal of the General Land Office to be hereunto affixed.

(SEAL)

GIVEN under my hand, at the City of Washington, the twenty-first day of August , in the year of our Lord one thousand nine hundred and seven, and of the Independence of the United States the one hundred and thirty-second.

By the President: *Theodore Roosevelt,*

By *F. M. McKean,* Secretary.

H. W. Sanford,

Recorder of the General Land Office.

This is a typical land patent issued under the Homestead act that has No federal conditions and stipulations delegating the exclusive Legislative authority to Congress meaning it is taxable by the state and not kept in exclusive federal jurisdiction.

Ben was finding plenty of information but few sources could explain the mineral patents that were obviously different than normal land patents.

He read on about how someone might own property that has natural gas, gold, or quartz in the ground and while the landowner might not have the means to dig up and capitalize on those assets or any interest in embarking on such an endeavor an oil or mining company with the appropriate equipment and knowledge might be eager to do so. Similarly, miners might not want to pay full market price for expensive real estate that happens to lie above a geological cache of natural resources but they might be willing to sign a 10 year lease that allows them to drill down and extract those resources from beneath the surface. Ben thought about the value of the mineral rights concerning the giant J which would require more research but it appeared that the value would be very hard to determine without some testing by an expert or two.

When companies have tapped a mine they can pull up their stakes and move to another leased location, without having to worry about buying and selling the entire site.

In such situations the respective parties strike a deal that is carefully spelled out in a legal contract known as a mineral rights agreement. A mineral rights transaction can involve all of the various minerals beneath the property, or can be restricted to specific commodities. Sometimes investors or brokers will even acquire rights to minerals that they have no intention of extracting, as an investment they can sell or lease to someone else. The possibilities are limitless, as is the potential for problems for those who do not have clearly worded and intelligently structured mineral rights contracts.

For instance, a rancher and a miner might think that they have a solid agreement that is mutually beneficial. But when extraction begins the miner sets off dynamite. The rancher's frightened cattle stampede, destroying crops and fences and injuring themselves. The upset rancher expects the miner to pay for damages, but the miner feels that it was his legal right to blast through rocks to extract his minerals. Before the end of the day the two adversaries are locked in an expensive old-fashioned feud.

A good mineral rights agreement helps to avoid such scenarios by covering every possible contingency and clearly outlining the method and time frame for extraction.

Keep in mind that those who purchase surface rights or buy a tract of land with the intention of owning and enjoying it in its entirety may be bound by previous mineral rights transfers or lease agreements.

Even if rights to subsurface assets were sold or leased decades ago they may still be enforceable. For that reason it is important to research the chain of ownership and ensure that the transfer of property awards all of the precious mineral rights without any unexpected restrictions.

Today we have state-of-the-art mining technologies and an insatiable global demand for subsurface minerals. Perhaps more now than at any other time in history, comprehensive mineral rights agreements between landowners and miners are essential for the protection and preservation of investments both above and below the surface of the land.

If good fences make good neighbors, excellent mineral rights agreements make great landowner and mining enterprise partnerships.

A few days later Ben received a call back from Rick Wilson Assistant Chief of Title Matters for the United States in the land acquisition division of (DOJ) Department of Justice.

Rick Wilson said he heard about the Andrew Jackson relation and thanked Ben for the country.

Ben was caught off guard but managed to respond with a nonchalant "yeah right no problem". Rick

was very helpful with encouraging Ben to get the situation straightened out in court. Rick was not able

to offer official legal advice but do to the uniqueness of the situation and military involvement

concerning Colonel Jackson he felt inclined to see if the United States had any interest in the situation

or could help direct Ben in the right direction. The conversations were short but Ben had several

conversations with Rick Wilson and Rick had even recommended that the DA sit sown and fix the

issue but the DA said he wasn't going to to sue himself and his job was to protect the county.

Ben received notice that he was being sued for clouding the Title of the tax owner on file and so

he hired a lawyer to defend his property ownership.

The bottom line is that the county sold the giant J illegally for taxes that should have never been

assessed in the first place starting another chain of title.

The giant J is federal jurisdiction and is in the middle of a national forest. What the hell is the county

Sheriff doing in the middle of federal jurisdiction? Ben explained the situation to his lawyer and the

defense was prepared.

They decided to counter claim that the county's illegal tax sale also led to the destruction of the historical building and the property is federal jurisdiction.

The week the case was scheduled for court Ben got a call from his lawyer Sue Parker who said that she had talked with judge Delmonte and the laws in the patent don't make the property federal jurisdiction and that his ancestors paid taxes on the property and that she could provide copies of the receipts. Ben said that was a lie and that his family never did pay taxes and that any receipts would be as fraudulent as the county's chain of title.

Then his own lawyer said that his chain of title was not a clear and valid title. Ben said what? It is the only chain of title starting from the original owner of the patent Colonel Jackson & Co who left it to his granddaughter and then it was deeded to Ben.

The county's chain of title had 11 owners in the chain and the Seventh Day Adventists Church was listed as one of the owners half way through the chain. The current owner John Longhorn had purchased the property from Mr. and Mrs. Gamez and appeared to have a mortgage on the property. The case went to court in late June 2010 and Ben waited patiently for justice to be served. The judge apparently disagreed with his counter complaint completely and even said that it was not federal jurisdiction and that he had the right to decide a federal question.

Ben had thoroughly verified the laws in the patent and yes it was federal jurisdiction. He was infuriated and immediately called Rick Wilson in Washington DC at DOJ to tell him what happened.

Rick's response was that the judge should be arrested for not upholding the federal law and that his

lawyer needed to file a complaint with the US Attorney General due to corruption at the county.

The following week Ben's lawyer basically said she would not go to federal court and that she

was retiring from law in the Black Hills but would send a complaint on the file to the US Attorney

General for review. Ben was annoyed but said he would find another lawyer to go to federal court.

His lawyer had mentioned the appeal process was only 30 days long but Ben didn't care because

he was not going to spend another dime in state court. If the state judge is not going to uphold the

federal law then maybe a federal judge would be more inclined to do so.

Ben was having a very difficult time finding a lawyer in the relatively sparsely populated area

that had any knowledge of federal mineral rights.

The next thing he knows Ben is reading an article about how a judge was being removed from

the bench for the first time in 121 years in the history of South Dakota.

An article was released in the newspaper about how the judge violated 3 out 4 judicial codes and that

he was law partners with Ben's judge prior to them both getting elected as judges.

Not only that these judges were the lawyers for Homestake Mine the largest gold mine in the world prior to becoming judges.

Ben could not believe what he was reading. Talk about corruption. If anybody knew mineral law it was these 2 judges. Ben was informed shortly after that his judge Delmonte was announcing retirement.

Was judge Delmonte being forced to retire because these guys were busted covering up mineral theft?

He was informed by the broker that Homestake Mine had leased the mineral rights in 1988 for exploration but didn't actually dig.

Ben realized that the judges were actually the lawyers for Homestake when the giant J was leased in the 80's. Ben started feeling really uncomfortable about the monster of corruption he was up against and had very little idea that it was this insane.

He also read on Wikipedia that Homestake killed everyone that didn't sell their federal mineral patents and acquired the rest of them through the court system illegally obviously by buying them in illegal county tax sales for pennies of the dollar.

His stomach began turning and feeling sick as he looked out the window of his office.

He wondered how deep this went and were these judges covering up more than just property theft in real time. A judge signed off on all these illegal chains of title in the 1930's and Ben was told that they did this to all of the mineral patents most likely. One lawyer said that if what he was saying is true then this situation is huge. As a sales engineer in the manufacturing industry Ben had became use to paying close attention to details on the complex projects he had worked on so when looking at federal laws written in his federal mineral patent he could obviously tell they were important and written for a reason.

Several months went by and Ben was told by Rick Wilson that a federal investigation was most likely underway. The year of 2011 seemed to have left him in a time warp and Ben was just waiting for something to happen while being told to get a new lawyer by the DOJ. By this point all the lawyers in real estate were saying they had a conflict of interest due to the fact that they all just realized that they represented someone who owns one of these mineral patents through an illegal chain of title started by the county and upheld by corrupt judges.

All he could do is sit back and wait for the federal government to force the state into following the federal law or try and hire a lawyer that was willing to go against the corrupt county and it's judges which was proving to be near impossible. Several lawyers said they wanted $25,000 as a retainer but could not guarantee justice in any way. Rick Wilson recommended that he try and get another federal agency to make a recommendation to the US Attorney.

Ben had already realized that the BLM who actually had jurisdiction of the property were in complete denial that it was their responsibility so Ben decided to ask the Forest Service for help who

had jurisdiction of all the land surrounding the giant J.

He also filed a complaint with the Inspector General's office of the Army and the Departmet of the

Interior.

After that he began contacting national law firms who operated nationwide but did not have a

conflict of interest because they were not local. Ben soon realized that the theft of these mineral

properties had been occurring all over the country in counties west of the Mississippi where mining

was common and especially in the national forest areas.

Rick Wilson the Title Chief had even said that the county was not going to fix the situation because

then they might have to fix all the other mineral properties they had stolen through illegal tax sales.

According to a 1956 Department of Justice report there has been an on going jurisdictional

conflict regarding this very matter of private property located in federal jurisdiction.

After talking to many big corporate gold mining lawyers it was clear that this illegal tax sales

scam of the nations mineral wealth was important to them because they had obviously taken advantage

of this jurisdictional loophole. They probably figured that even if someone did figure it out someday

they would have already mined the property and acquired the gold. The farther Ben dug into the situation he could see that many of the properties sold in tax sales had been mined or explored and many had been rolled into real estate portfolios and being sold as vacation retreats with no mention whatsoever of the federal mineral rights in the ads. It was big mess! If the gold mining companies hadn't illegally acquired the mineral patents through the illegal tax sales then you can bet the real estate people were trying to market them as awesome vacation spots.

Bottom line is they are all trespassing on private property and have no right to the property under federal law which the state and county are ignoring.

Ben compared it to owning a jewelry store and getting robbed on a daily basis by trespassers. What's the difference when they are trespassing on our gold mine he would say to the lawyers?

It was difficult to say if the government was going to do something or not and his father was very skeptical that anything would get fixed in the midst of all the corruption. Ben spent weeks on the phone with various lawyers all over the country. Most of the lawyers had no idea what he was talking about regarding federal jurisdiction. Some of the big gold mining companies had acknowledged the federal jurisdiction of the mineral patents but seemed very hesitant and reserved when considering that there was no property tax and they were basically "Federal Enclaves" where only Congress has legislative authority to make rules on the premises.

Obviously these big companies have an interest in controlling the gold market and acquiring all

of the valuable mineral patents at pennies on the dollar in illegal tax sales which was certainly a quick

way to run a monopoly on all the mineral assets. Ben was also told by a real estate broker that his giant

J gold mine had been leased in the mid 1980's by Homestake the largest gold mine in the world but

they only explored and didn't mine anything. The thought of somebody stealing the family property and

destroying his family fort was really disturbing and kept eating away at his nerves. Ben was beginning

to realize that his ownership of a giant J goldmine was a reality and that he was under attack from a

corrupt state government.

War was not anything that Ben wanted to consider in reality but was obviously a common topic when

talking about the family and extended families of Andrew and Stonewall Jackson.

Continuing the legal search was turning up nothing of any comfort whatsoever. Finley and Klug

said they wanted $25,000 to even look at the case which seemed like a relatively common response as

he sorted through the online attorney directory.

In between phone calls he would strum a few chords on the guitar and either work on his most

recent songs or just think about the days of cowboys and Indians.

Finally after many failure calls he was able to get some decent responses from lawyers outside the Black Hills area. Marston, Crandall, and Gresch said that the situation was beyond the scope of a normal lawyer and that the US Attorney would most likely do something about it eventually. A local lawyer said the situation is huge and pretty much the same thing. The frustrating thing is that Ben can only sit and wait for the slow wheels of government which could take years like Rick Wilson said. One of Ben's friends had mentioned that the judge being removed is unprecedented and is obviously a sign that something is being done. Rick Wilson had even told Ben that the state and federal judicial system is connected and regulated from the top levels of government. Most likely someone pretty high up the ladder had approved the removal of a judge even if it was a state judge.

Ben also made a number of calls to his cousins in Tennessee including Andrew Jackson VI an active judge in Knoxville,TN. Ben explained the situation and Andy said that he needed a new lawyer and a federal review and told Ben to keep him posted on the progress of the situation.

Ben began researching the federal laws and the constitutional rights that have been violated which in this case was done by the state and county governments.

The constitution of the United States declares that congress shall have power to exercise "exclusive legislation" in all "cases whatsoever" over all places purchased by the consent of the legislature of the state in which the same shall be, for the erection of forts, magazines, arsenals, dockyards and other needful buildings. When therefore a purchase of land for any of these purposes is

made by the national government, and the state legislature has given its consent to the purchase, the

land so purchased by the very terms of the constitution falls within exclusive legislation of

congress, and the state jurisdiction is completely ousted.

Ben could see that Congress had clearly explained why there might be a jurisdictional question over an

area and "exclusive legislation" in all "cases whatsoever" over all places purchased by the consent of

the legislature of the state. Most States, in their desire to facilitate Federal construction within

their borders, enacted statutes consenting to the acquisition of land and these general consent statutes

had the effect of granting the United States exclusive jurisdiction over lands so acquired.

*While these enclaves, which are used for all the many Federal governmental purposes, such as post offices, arsenals, dams; road; etc., usually are owned by the Government, **the United States in many cases has received similar jurisdictional authority over privately owned properties which it leases, or privately owned and occupied properties which are located within the exterior boundaries of a large area (such as the District of Columbia and various national parks) as to which a State has ceded jurisdiction to the United States***.

this is the stipulation #6 in the mineral patent
Section 2338 (U. S. Comp. Stat. 1901, p. 1436) reads as follows: As a condition of sale, in the absence of necessary legislation by Congress, the local legislature of any state or territory may provide rules for working mines, involving easements, drainage, and other necessry means to their complete development; and those conditions shall be fully expressed in the patent.'

It should be emphasized that Federal instrumentalities and their property are not in any event subject to State or local taxation or to most types of State or local control. However, the transfer to the United States of exclusive legislative jurisdiction over an area has the effect, speaking generally, of divesting the State and any governmental entities operating under its authority of any right to tax or control private persons or property upon the area.
b) Taxable Possessory Interests. "Taxable possessory interests" are possessory interests in publicly-owned real property. Excluded from the meaning of "taxable possessory interests", however, are any possessory interests in real property located within an area to which the United States has exclusive jurisdiction concerning
taxation. Such areas are commonly referred to as federal enclaves.

In an ensuing study of the State supreme court decision with a view toward applying to the Supreme Court of the United States for a writ of certiorari, the Department of Justice ascertained that State laws and practices relating to the subject of Federal legislative jurisdiction are very different in different States, that practices of Federal agencies with respect to the same subject vary extremely from agency to agency without apparent basis, and that the Federal Government, the States, residents of Federal areas, and other; are all suffering serious disabilities and disadvantages because of a general lack of knowledge or understanding of the subject of Federal legislative jurisdiction and its consequences.

Although government promotes itself endlessly as our indispensable "protector" and principle guardian of our Constitutional Rights, it's not true. Nevertheless, that self-promotion has effectively conditioned most Americans to believe our Constitutional Rights are respected and vigorously protected by government and public servants. Unfortunately, only a few people realize that government does not automatically protect our Rights, that our inclination to trust government is dangerously misguided, and that our ignorance of our Rights encourages government to abuse those Rights.

The relationship between any government and its citizens is, and has always been, at best,

ADVERSARIAL: individual Rights are inversely proportional to government power. The more power the government has, the fewer Rights you have. Government can't grow in size or power except at the cost of our individual Rights and freedom. The founding fathers also realized that all governments seek to expand their powers and are therefore driven to diminish their citizen's Rights. Hence, the Constitution was written to both limit government and maximize our individual Rights.

In reality the American Constitution is essentially an anti-government document.

The Constitution's principle purpose is not simply to specify our individual Rights, but to shield us from the single organization that will always pose the greatest threat to those Rights: our own government. That's why we have three branches of government, checks and balances, elections every two years, the opportunity to call constitutional conventions, the Right to jury trials, and the Right to keep and bear arms and each political mechanism was designed to empower the public to restrict government and thereby to protect the people against government's inevitable urge to tyranny.

If the principle enemy of any people is their own government, and if the principle defender of the American people is the American Constitution, then it follows that the first enemy of our government is our Constitution. Government understands this conflict, but tries to conceal it from the public by claiming to be the only interpreter and protector of the Constitution. But if only the government interprets the Constitution, then those interpretations are typically biased to empower government --

the Constitution's archenemy -- at the expense of the people.

Given the conflict between government and our Constitution, it follows that:
1) The government is not interested in protecting the Constitution;

2) Although the government uses the Constitution to legitimize itself, it's principle interest is in

DESTROYING the Constitution; and 3) That the only party able to truly protect and defend YOUR

Rights is YOU.

Sound far-fetched? It's not. Even the courts agree.

The individual Rights guaranteed by our Constitution can be compromised or ignored by our

government. For example, in US. vs.Johnson (76 Fed Supp. 538), Federal District Court Judge James

Alger Fee ruled that,

"The privilege against self-incrimination is neither accorded to the passive resistant, nor to the

person who is ignorant of his rights, nor to one indifferent thereto. It is a FIGHTING clause. It's

benefits can be retained only by sustained COMBAT. It cannot be claimed by attorney or solicitor. It is

valid only when insisted upon by a BELLIGERENT claimant in person."

Knights of the Golden Circle
Chapter 5

Ben noted his family in the military going back to the Revolutionary war and to the 13 colonies

along the east coast. May 1, 1815: The U.S. Army reorganizes and downsizes following the end of the

War of 1812. Major General Andrew Jackson, a former Tennessee Militia commander and fresh off

his decisive victory at the Battle of New Orleans, retains his rank as six other Major

Generals and 12 Brigadier Generals are reduced in rank, making him the second

highest ranking officer in the U.S. Army and reporting directly to the Secretary of War.

In May 6, 1861 the Tennessee General Assembly passed a "Declaration of Independence" and approved secession subject to ratification and a popular referendum that took place on June 8 which

passed 104,000 to 47,000. The Tennessee Militia was no longer subject to the Militia Act of 1792 and

would soon be placed under control of the Confederate States of America.

Ben was reading a book written by Bob Brewer and Warren Getler called "Shadow of the

Sentinel". Bob Brewer is considered to be a KGC expert and was the adviser on the Book Of Secrets

treasure movie. Ben found the book fascinating and kept it around like a dictionary when referencing

the KGC, Freemasons, or Jesse James. Ben had called the Newspaper that wrote an article about

Bob and acquired the email address for him. They began chatting via email occasionally and Bob was

certainly a well respected name in the treasure hunting community as Ben had learned during his

archeology studies and researching many confederate treasure stories and areas across the country.

Ben asked detailed questions about the KGC and tried to narrow down what happened to them and

where the gold might be that is missing from the giant J property.

According to Bob, the south had won the war and the KGC was easily the most powerful spy network

to ever operate in the United States. Ben learned that there were many KGC depositories created where

the gold was buried up until the 1916 time frame which is about when Grandpa Jackson had retired.

At this point Ben had a little secret that he wasn't sharing with anybody until more evidence could be obtained to support his theory. He had asked Bob about Jesse James and according to Bob's

book the legendary outlaw had become the Colonel and Commander of KGC. Bob said his book is

really all he has on old Jesse and that there were over 300 books written about him and many movies.

He said don't believe everything you hear about Jesse James good or bad. He said there are so many

half truths and stories regarding him that its impossible to tell what is real for sure.

Bob's book says that what history has failed to realize is that Jesse Robert James from Missouri

was born in 1847 in Clay County but that name never surfaced when the KGC faked the death of the

real Jesse Woodson James who was from Kentucky or Tennessee. J. Frank Dalton was a man that came

forward in the 1940's and was reported in several newspapers claiming that he was the real Jesse

Woodson James. Bob didn't believe that J. Frank Dalton was really Jesse W J ames but Bob did

confirm several claims of Dalton to be true like locations of KGC depositories.

Bob Brewer is one of the few KGC treasure hunters who have actually found several hundred thousand

dollars worth of gold and silver coins considered to be buried KGC treasure or payroll caches. Certain

facts regarding these locations were known by Dalton and also certain facts regarding the real JWJ. The

problem with Dalton's story though was that many of his facts were proven to be completely false or

sketchy at best. Even still many people were convinced that J. Frank Dalton was the real Jesse W.

James.

Dalton said that JRJ and JWJ were first cousins and comrades in arms during and after the civil war.

Another theory floating around was that Dalton was actually truly a KGC operative and was releasing information for a reason. Many speculated that he was using Confederate codes in his story so that the descendants of the KGC would know how to find the treasures if they had been left with certain valuable information unknowingly.

There was a journalist named John Newman Edwards at the Kansas City Times who was almost fully responsible for creating the knight-gallant "Robin Hood" image of the James Gang through his collective editorials. In his most familiar "Chivalry of Crime" article in the Kansas City Times, Edwards went on to say that men "with the halo of medieval chivalry upon their garments". The medieval reference may suggest an association with the James Gang and the KGC and the Knights Templar.

Shadow of the Sentinel by Bob Brewer spoke about how the KGC used mining companies as fronts for KGC activities because mining could easily mask the elaborate vaults and shafts deigned to bury the treasures.

Apparently the KGC hauled massive Confederate treasure hoards to depositories all over the wild western frontier in the post civil war era between 1866 and the 1890's.

Bob said according to J. Frank Dalton the cousins theory appeared to be correct based on his research and that there were at least 2 Jesse James and maybe even 3 or 4. Dalton's story had spun off a bunch of new theories but nobody knew what to believe anymore by the 1940's and Jesse James whoever he was was probably dead for real by the 1940's anyway.

Ben had a feeling that the truth about the KGC and the treasure was probably centered around and connected to the mystery of Jesse James.

The J. Frank Dalton Story is pretty much at the pinnacle of "Jesse James Was One of His Names" by Del Schrader.

The highly controversial book published in 1975 was a wonder of historical potentialities and big time assertions.

Ben noted that at the heart of the claims is that Jesse Woodson James was a post-civil war leader of the Knights of the Golden Circle and that the KGC's main goal after completely going under ground was to prepare for a second civil war. The book has been out of print and greatly sought after by treasure hunters, Jesse James and KGC historians, and Civil War enthusiasts goes into substantial detail to explain the secret organization of the KGC. The book covers many changes throughout the

KGC's post civil war evolution which include the owning of major businesses, railroads, mining and timber operations, banks, racehorses as front companies for sources of operating revenue.

The legitimate accuracy of the J. Frank Dalton Story remains open to further discussion and analysis.

Dalton-James life as told in Jesse James Was One of His Names is told in the voice of of someone going by the name Jesse James III. The person whose legal name was Orvus Lee Howk also went by the name Jesse Lee James and claimed to have been a grandson of Jesse Woodson James.

Jesse Lee James aka Orvus Lee Howk spent his lifetime as a detective and bodyguard-confidant -executor for his notorious grandfather.

The real interesting thing to Ben was that he now knows that his cousin Lt General Stonewall Jackson was 2nd in command of the entire Confederate Army and if anyone knew about the KGC's agenda and activities it was probably Stonewall's extended family.

Ben thought about Stonewall and how he was killed supposedly by friendly fire. Ben thought about how his cousin General Andrew Jackson had been the first President to almost be assassinated. The gunman pulled 2 guns and fired them at point blank but they both misfired. Talk about divine intervention he thought and wondered why Stonewall wasn't so lucky. The fallout of Stonewalls death was considered a devastating blow to the entire Confederacy. General Robert E. Lee said he had lost his right arm when Stonewall was killed.

Ben wondered what his family must have felt and how they dealt with such a loss. It occurred to Ben that his family may have been involved with the KGC since it appears that secrecy within the Confederacy was probably severely enforced after Stonewall was killed.

Ben thought about how those soldiers could be so stupid that they would shoot their own General. Ben had found that there were threats of deserters and actual deserters causing problems with rank and file and so Stonewall had ordered 6 of them to be placed in front of the firing squad. Ben felt pretty confident that Stonewall's death was quite possibly not an accident at all and that the North was really the aggressor in the war which ironically many southerners had also called it the war of "Northern Aggression". It was clear that the war was a financial war and slavery was just a product of the plantation economy which the south had primarily controlled although there were northern slave states and plantations as well.

It crossed Ben's mind that the KGC's payback for his cousin Stonewall's death was ultimately the assassination of President Lincoln who started the war. John Wilkes Booth was apparently a member of the White Camellia's that was ultimately controlled by the KGC.

Then Ben thought about the apparent assassination of Jesse James and the ridiculous irony of the situation. It appears that the Union army got Stonewall killed whether intentionally or not which led to

the KGC killing Lincoln and then the leader of the KGC gets assassinated in 1882 over a decade after

the war was supposedly over. It's basically a revolving door of payback Ben though to himself but

something didn't add up. If the KGC was the most powerful spy network to ever operate in the USA

then how could some miniscule players like Bob and Charlie Ford get away with killing the

Commander of the KGC. How could they even expect to get away with it? Something did not add up

and Ben was leaning towards the mythical theory that Jesse James faked his death in 1882.

Ben figured between 1882 and 1916 the KGC mystery and Jesse James

mystery most likely were connected and interwoven with each other.

Ben had done his fair share of genealogy research by now and decided to pull up the 1850

census for Jesse James. If you look at the 1850 federal census you will see very clearly Jesse R James

listed as 4 years old. It appears that Bob was right and the Jesse James that lived in Missouri was

named Jesse Robert James after his father Robert. Ben had just uncovered his first major clue and

indication that Jesse W James did in fact fake his death. It appears that J. frank Dalton was also correct

when he said that the name Jesse Robert James never even surfaced in 1882. The next strange thing he

noticed was that the 1860 census had been clearly altered with an ink pen in an attempt to alter the middle initial R into a W which actually looks more like an H but it has definitely been tampered with

and even shows an ink pen mark to the left of the column that matched the ink on the altered initial R.

It appeared someone had made an attempt to alter the federal census to indicate that Jesse W James was

from Clay County Missouri just like everyone had been saying in 1870. Dalton said that JRJ went

to Canada and JWJ went to the far west to hide out during the 1882 hoax.

According to several other reports and forensic studies the guy in the casket was a man named

Charlie Bigelow who was going around using Jesse James name during the robberies or it was a cousin

with similar features named Jesse M. James who fit the bill for the KGC cover up perfectly.

Ben had seen a J symbol used on KGC treasure maps but Bob Brewer had said that they didn't

really look like the capitalized Giant J on Ben's map. The lower case j had been seen on several KGC

maps and some supposedly being made by Jesse James himself.

If the guy in Missouri was his cousin then who was the real Jesse Woodson James and how old

was he in reality. That was another question that many people have thought they knew the answer to

but were apparently wrong. Jesse R James from Missouri was only a teenager during the civil war and

the KGC was active during the civil war and documented by the union.

There were raids during the civil war behind union lines that were attributed to the KGC. It is doubtful

Ben thought that the Jesse R James form Missouri had any command over those civil war raids because he was just a teenager. Also many of the reports after the civil war were of a man over 6 ft tall that described Jesse James but the Jesse R James from Missouri was 5 ft 8 inches tall.

Some researchers had thought Dalton may have been using Confederate codes and Ben had verified so far that at least some of what he said was true. Ben wondered if the vast treasure stories that Dalton spoke of were real as well but he figured the truth was probably protected by the same KGC members that helped fake the death of the real Jesse James.

Ben's great great grandpa Jackson was born in 1866 so he certainly could not be the real Jesse W James that served in the civil war. Ben's secret that he'd been keeping to himself is that he had stumbled across a file of the Confederate Veteran Pension list in Tennessee. As he looked for his 3rd great grandpa George Washington Jackson he noticed that he was listed with wife Rebecca James Jackson. It was the only Rebecca and George on the list.

The chart that his cousin Tony England had done in Tennessee had Rebecca's last name incorrect which Ben had not noticed before nor did it seem important. Ben had a feeling that somehow his grandpa Jackson's mother was related to the real Jesse Woodson James.

Ben thought she was probably a cousin to Jesse James possibly which would make grandpa

Jackson a cousin but there is no way to know for sure until he found the real family for Rebecca James before she married into the Jackson clan.

Ben had read that Jesse Woodson James robbed more banks and trains than anyone in history in order to fill the KGC coffers between 1866 and at least 1882. There were reports of KGC activities after his apparently faked death in 1882 but most of the public considered him dead. So the Brad Pitt movie called the Assassination of Jesse James was not historically accurate in several ways.

Ben thought that this giant J story is already a movie but if he could figure out the truth about Jesse James then that would be an incredible addition to an already amazing story.

A relatively rare article had said Jesse James traded the Sioux plains tribes repeating rifles and guerrilla warfare training for 2 wagon loads of gold and access to the Black Hills. The article said the great Sioux leader Sitting Bull himself had made the agreement and the KGC was known for signing up the Native American tribes into the Confederacy. Jesse James was known for operating in Indian country but this was also 10 years after the civil war in 1876.

Certain members of the KGC were also Cherokee and Choctaw friends that helped make those native alliances as well. The battle of Little Bighorn was a defiant victory against General Custer and the 7th cavalry of the US Army. The Indians were armed with repeating rifles and also heavily outnumbered the approaching army. Ben read as much on Jesse James as he could and found out that

he was also active in Mexico and the southwest areas of New Mexico and Texas. Some articles put his

headquarters in the Far Northwest possibly in Northern California.

Apparently the KGC operated over the entire country by the1880's and Jesse James had even made an

alliance with the Mexican Emperor Maximilian and was paid 5 million dollars for escorting him to

safety during a revolt.

Jesse James had become one of the wealthiest most powerful men in the country and yet he was

supposedly dead.

Studying the signs,symbols, and ways of the Masons was intriguing and seemed to hold some

type of hidden knowledge in more ways than one.

The KGC apparently used an elaborate Confederate code system to bury payroll money for the army

during the civil war and KGC depositories for the Confederate treasury. Ben had seen the Jesse James

symbol of JJ in several documented apparent KGC hotspots in Oklahoma and the deep south. Many of

the treasure markers or symbols used by the KGC were of various animals or tracks. Turkey tracks and

turtles were big indicators that you were in a potential KGC depository area. Terrapins were very high

on the pecking order for KGC treasure markers. If you find a turtle or a j there is usually gold near by.

The letter j was also used in some of the supposedly authentic treasure maps that have surfaced over the years but none that looked like the giant J. Ben had thought that the giant J actually looked like a stone carving of a backwards capital J connected to a regular capital J carving that looks almost like an anchor or a letter W located in Oklahoma. The carving has been interpreted as being made by the Outlaw Jesse Woodson James.

According to the KGC experts Jesse Woodson James was a 33rd degree master mason just like Benjamin Franklin, Andrew Jackson, and George Washington. Many have speculated that Albert Pike who was also a 33rd degree master mason and Confederate General was possibly the most powerful Scottish Rite Freemason in the world and was involved in the designing of the KGC depository systems.

One thing that was shrouded in mystery was the fact that Jesse James was apparently an outlaw at the same time that he was supposedly an active field commander for the KGC who had not given up the war. It was pretty clear that the outlaw wasn't just robbing banks, trains, and stagecoaches for his own greedy means. Jesse James was filling the KGC depositories for when the south would rise again. Jesse Woodson James was the last rebel Colonel who against all odds was still active and engaging in guerilla warfare behind enemy lines even though the war was over according to the official headlines. Lincoln who had started the war was now dead. The KGC was systematically eliminating all threats and beginning to organize a new financial structure that would be controlled solely by them obviously.

The KGC treasure grids were laid out with coded symbols in the forest or terrain that would point to another symbol or a treasure. Often several of these symbols would be laid out miles apart but where the lines intersect is where you want to dig. Ben was looking for intersecting lines? The KGC map called Solomon's Temple showed a circle that was enclosed inside a square on a 45 degree angle with intersecting lines at many 45 degree angles. Ultimately the KGC ran heard on pretty much every

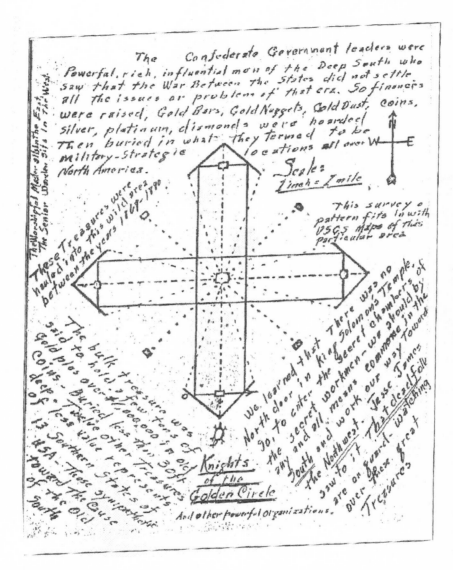

group that ever operated in a military or political capacity in the south. Jesse W James also worked

very closely with the Cherokee Confederate Brigadier General Stand Watie who was in command of

the Indian Brigades including Chickasaw, Choctaw, and several other plains tribes.

A lot of men were killed during the War Between the States. It was brutal out there and it was neighbor against neighbor. It was horrible. These guys were the product of all that.

Jesse Woodson James operated a spy network and in the beginning there were more of them because they had just come out of the war. They had all fought as guerillas. So they were very well seasoned soldiers. Not just punks off the street going out robbing banks. These were ex-Confederate soldiers, well seasoned in warfare. When they went in to rob a bank, it was a quasi-military operation."

Cole Younger, a member of the James Gang was asked if they were bad men and he said, 'We were rough men. We were used to rough ways. But I will tell you this. We never violated the sanctity of a man's home. We never robbed the honest poor. We always treated ladies with respect and when we came into a town, every man knew our business'. So yes, they were rough guys but they weren't common thugs. They were articulate, many were well educated, and they all fought as soldiers in the biggest war in US history.

The KGC evolved from a Scottish secret group known as The Society of the Horseman's Word, otherwise known as the Horse Whisperers. This fraternity recited passages from the Bible backwards and practiced folk magic as part of their rituals, in addition to having Masonic-style oaths.

Headquarters for the Knights of the Golden Circle was 814 Fatherland Dr. in Nashville. This was the home of KGC operative Frank James, elder brother of Jesse Woodson James. Years later it became the Dixie Tabernacle, original home of the Grand Ole Opry.

The KGC claimed 200,000 members all over America during the war. All of the men in Lincoln's cabinet were Knights. The KGC was heavily financed by the London and Paris Rothschild brothers/Knights Templars.

Their goal was to foment as much chaos and discord as possible in order to keep the country divided and to usher in a Rothschild/Templar-owned central bank.

But Lincoln had his own plans. During his presidency his 50% tariff jump-started the American steel industry while his railroads, subsidies for mining, free land for farmers and free state colleges transformed a bankrupt cotton-exporting country into the world's greatest industrial power within 25 years. Lincoln knew that he was waging a separate but equally brutal war against Rothschild/Templar dominated Wall St. firms with his attempt at reasserting government control of credit. He put through anti-usury and other strict banking laws, sold bonds directly to the people and issued hundreds of millions of national currency.

With these reforms The Great Emancipator had signed his own death warrant.

Lincoln knew that his time was short. He confided to his bodyguard Ward Lamont a week before he

was killed that he had a vision of his own death.

According to a sworn statement by "Wild Bill" Lincoln: Our branch of the Lincoln family was never

satisfied with what really happened to Booth, and I spent fourteen years of my life running down the

true story. Strangely enough, I learned it from Jesse W. James, head of the Confederate underground. I

was present at Booth's real death. Jesse James and "Wild Bill" Lincoln allegedly crept into Booth's

room at the Grand Avenue Hotel in Enid, Oklahoma, then tricked the hungover Booth into drinking

arsenic-laced lemonade. Booth is said to have died in their presence. Although commonly reported that

Booth's corpse was mummified by direction of his lawyer, Finis Bates, some claim it was the massive

arsenic in Booth's system which caused the mummification. James reportedly arranged for Booth's

body to be exhibited on tour, throughout the United States. According to Schrader, Booth's mummified

remains eventually passed into the ownership of a Minnesota jeweler named Jay Gould, relative of the

notorious banker. Today, the whereabouts of the Booth mummy are unknown.

The Confederate government went underground in 1865, and was headquartered in Nashville until about 1884. The South's spy network was very good.

How did the Confederacy stave off defeat during "The War of Northern Aggression," four long years, 1861-1865? The answer in part, says KGC analysts, is that the South had a better spy network and that spy network did not just go away in 1865. Feeling in the South still simmered and boiled against the "damn Yankees" after 1865. When those "damn Yankees" increased their war upon the Indian nations of the American West, many southerners strongly sympathized with the Indians. To Jesse James, "Sitting Bull, Chief Joseph, and other chiefs were Confederate allies.

There was an organization called The Grange, not generally discussed, called the Patriots of Husbandry today. Similar to a fraternal organization it was started after the Civil War when the government, through eminent domain allowed the railroad to take possession of private property. It upset the farmers and to protect themselves they banded together in an organization called The Grange of which Frank and Jesse James were members. They fought the railroads tooth and nail so it was no myth that Jesse James was the champion of the farmer and the farmers joined The Grange by the thousands. In 1875, there were thousands of members nationwide with strong membership in the South. Jesse James became the hero of the farmers and the story of Jesse fighting the trains and banks comes down from this Grange movement. Jesse James did not invent striking back at the railroad that was a common feeling among many folks during that time. Jesse just happened to be articulating it with arms and guerilla warfare. That's why to this day Jesse James is a hero to the common man and the average American can identify with Jesse James and is why the south will always say he was a Robin Hood. But the fact of the matter is that he's more than a Robin Hood. Jesse James embodies the things that Americans treasure most in individuality and the boldness ability to be brave, and daring, and to stand up for what you believe. People don't really see the bank robberies, they see that part of Jesse James that's in all Americans and his devoted fight against corruption over the theft of peoples family property and lively hood. Similar to most political groups of the old south and post war era the KGC ultimately rode heard on all of them that were of any significance.

Ben could not help but recognize a direct similarity between himself and Jesse James. Why was he being forced to fight the government and it's corporate corruption. Why is this happening again in modern times? Will Ben be forced to go live in a cave like an outlaw on the run? The fact is that many peoples properties have been stolen and now Ben has prayed to his ancestors for help and direction. Will they get off Colonel Jackson's property? Is this still the America we thought it was?

There are too many questions that need answering.

Ben pulled up a written account from the state archives that mentioned the Black Hills state militia was under the command of Colonel Merritt H Day the entire time during the messiah war of 1890-91 and Colonel Day was also listed as the President of Colonel Jackson's gold mining company located on the giant J until retiring in 1894. Ben recounts the strategic military campaign of the Black Hills to determine how the KGC and Colonel Jackson's Tennessee militia were key elements of securing the gold fields.

As if drought and famine were not enough to try out the pioneers of the new state, the fall of 1890 brought to our very door a great Indian uprising which resulted in a vast tragedy. In a degree, this uprising was an incident of the drought, though it was in a greater measure predicated upon other circumstances. The extremely dry weather, however, had destroyed all the Indians' little efforts at agriculture and gardening with which they had for several years supplemented the rations issued to them by the government. Uncle Sam is not quick to adjust himself to changed conditions and it was difficult to make him understand at once why the rations which were sufficient in 1888 were not adequate in 1889 and 1890. The Indians had felt the pinch of hunger and were restive under the situation. At this juncture the South Dakota Sioux were visited by emissaries of tribes west of the Rocky mountains who, inspired by fanatical superstitions, represented to them that the Messiah of the

Indians was about to return to earth and restore the old free life, with game and buffalo in abundance, while the whites were to be driven from the earth. Early in November delegates were sent by the South Dakota bands to attend a gathering of choice spirits at Pyramid Lake in Utah, where it was represented that the Messiah was to appear. These delegates stole away from the agencies and made remarkable progress to Pyramid lake, where they met representatives of sixteen other tribes, some of them having traveled fourteen hundred miles to reach the rendezvous. It almost surpasses belief, but it is nevertheless true that these delegates called without telegraph or written message, had started from points a thousand miles remote from each other and had arrived at the rendezvous at the appointed time. There the pretended Messiah appeared to them and made to them great promises. The youth of all the older Indians was to be renewed so that no man among them would be more than forty years old. Everything was to be restored as it was in former times before the white men came. That medicine men would be sent among them to cure with a touch all of their wounds and sickness so that they would live forever. He then taught them to dance the ghost dance and sent them back to their tribes.

Short Bull, an Oglala, was the leader of the Dakota delegates. His home was at Pine Ridge. He was a hostile, or heathen Indian, as distinguished from the friendly fellows who thronged about the agency. He came home and at once began to teach the doctrines of the new Messiah to the chiefs and the dance to the young men. At first he told him all the mysterious changes would come in two seasons, but as the Indians took up the new doctrine and became frenzied in the dance, which they carried to the extreme, dancing for days in succession without rest or food until dropping down from sheer exhaustion, Short Bull, who at first was but a John the Baptist, announcing the coming of the Messiah, grew bolder and proclaimed his own divine and miraculous power. His first act was to set ahead the date of the uprising which was to be a preliminary to the grand restoration, one year, that is to the fall of 1890, which by this time was already at hand. He then commanded all the warriors to assemble in the Bad Lands on White river in November. While the dancing and excitement was largely confined to Pine Ridge, the Sioux at the other agencies were uneasy and inclined to listen to Short Bull's runners who were constantly among them. This is particularly true of the wild Indians belonging to the Cheyenne river agency, who lived back on Cherry creek, and the Uncpapas on upper Grand river. Almost immediately the Indians started for the Bad Lands, looting the homes of the farmer Indians as they went and forcing many peaceably inclined ones to join them. They made a camp near the mouth of Pass creek, where in a short time three thousand of the dancers were assembled. Dr. D. F. Royer, the agent at Pine Ridge, first became alarmed about the middle of the month and General Miles, in command of the department of the Northwest, had sent strong detachments of troops under General Brooke to Pine Ridge and Rosebud, but no general alarm was felt in the state until the 24th of

November when Scotty Philip came in from his ranch on Bad river to inform Governor Mellette that an outbreak was imminent at any moment. Governor Mellette telegraphed this information promptly to General Miles, who at once strengthened the force at the agencies and a cordon of troops were placed along the Cheyenne from the Forks up to the Elkhorn railway crossing and down that line toward Chadron as a protection to the Black Hills, and strong garrisons were posted at Forts Bennett and Sully and at Fort Yates. Little danger was apprehended from the Indians at Cheyenne river agency proper. In fact the leading Indians there could confidently be depended upon to assist in the protection of the frontier; but there was some cause for apprehension that the Uncpapas on Grand river who came under the direct personal influence of Sitting Bull, might make a dash across the river among the settlers, the force at Fort Yates was kept on the alert and Governor Mellette armed the militia in Walworth and Campbell counties and they were some time kept under marching orders under the command of Col. Thomas Orr. General Miles established his headquarters at Rapid City. The policy of the army was to force the Indians back to the agency without a conflict. To this end efforts were put forth to create dissensions among the Sioux themselves and so weaken their strength.

Among the Uncpapas it was believed that the chief disturber was old Sitting Bull himself and that if he could be placed under arrest, his followers would remain quietly at the agency, or at least upon the reservation and the excitement would soon die out. Sitting Bull had spent a season or two as an attraction in the Wild West show of "Buffalo Bill" Cody and General Miles was of the opinion that Cody would have greater influence with him than any other white man. Cody was therefore sent to Standing Rock to coax the old medicine man to come in on the 25th of November, but the Indians, suspecting his mission, sent the showman off on a fool's errand to find Sitting Bull at a point a long distance from where he actually was, and after chasing about in a vain hunt for him, Cody gave up the mission. This attempt to draw off the old disturber having failed, the war department, being unduly fearful of Sitting Bull's power, it was determined to arrest him at all hazards and the commandant at Fort Yates was instructed to effect his arrest without delay. Consequently on the evening of December 10th Major McLaughlin the agent at Standing Rock, selected a body of Indian police in whom he had confidence, to go out and make the arrest. They were to be supported by Captain Fechet with a detail of troops. Sitting Bull's home was in a substantial log house located on Grand river, in South Dakota, not far from the mouth of Rock creek and about thirty-five miles southwest of Standing Rock. The police, closely followed by the troops, left the agency about midnight, on the night of the 10th and made a rapid drive to Sitting Bull's where they arrived about four o'clock in the morning. The police arrived first and going directly to the house found the old man asleep in bed, they awakened him and told him their business and advised him to submit peaceably. He was indignant and raised a cry of revolt which speedily drew about him a strong force of his followers, who opened fire upon the police and a desperate fight ensued in which six of the policemen and Sitting Bull himself were killed. The hostiles were vastly in the majority and it is probable that the entire body of policemen would have been wiped out had not Captain Fechet arrived at the moment the fight was at its height and, quickly mounting a Hochkiss gun, soon drove back the hostiles and rescued the remaining policemen. Most of the remaining hostiles gave up at once, but some of them started for the Short Bull camp in the Bad Lands, but were intercepted on the Cheyenne, and, with the exception of thirty, who made their way to the White river, were placed under arrest and in a short time returned to Standing Rock. The hostile element among the Cheyenne river Indians were chiefly in the band of Hump, out on Cherry creek. Hump was considered to be particularly formidable and his location too was such that he made a strong link in the line of communication between the hostile Oglalas and the Uncpapas. Captain Ewers, of the Fifth Infantry, had during his residence at Fort Bennett, became a strong friend of Hump's. At this time

Ewers was stationed in Texas, but he was sent for and, proceeding to Fort Bennett, drove at once out to Hump's camp, sixty miles away, on Cherry creek, without troops and unarmed. Hump was twenty miles from home, but a runner went to him and he at once came in to see his old friend. Captain Ewers explained the situation to him and asked him to accompany him to Fort Bennett. To this Hump at once assented and took his people down to the fort, where they remained peaceably until the troubles were

over, Hump himself joining General Miles' forces and rendering effective service as a scout. One of

the sub-chiefs, however, did not come in, but started to join Short Bull. This was Big Foot, who with

certain scattered hostiles from the Cheyenne and Grand River, rounded up one hundred and sixteen

men and, though once apprehended by Captain Summers, they by a subterfuge evaded him. When

Colonel Sumner had intercepted Big Foot near the Cheyenne on December 22nd, he promised to return

with his people to the Cheyenne river agency, but on that night escaped and started south to join Short

Bull. This fact was at once communicated to headquarters and orders were telegraphed to General

Brooke at Pine Ridge to intercept Big Foot and place him and his warriors under arrest. In the

meantime Short Bull had become more reasonable and had determined to return to the agency, and on

the night of December 29th had arrived within six miles of Pine Ridge. On the 28th of December Major

Whiteside, under orders from General Brooke, met Big Foot and his band near Porcupine creek and

demanded his surrender. Big Foot and his band of one hundred and six warriors and their women and

children submitted without resistance. Ten others of Big Foot's warriors were out on a scout attempting

to locate the camp of Short Bull. After the arrest they moved over on to Wounded Knee creek and went

into camp. At this camp Major Whiteside was joined by Colonel Forsythe and Lieutenant Taylor with details of troops, so that in the aggregate they had four hundred and seventy fighting men. The next morning the scouting party of hostiles returned to camp and immediately the Indians opened fire upon the troops from short guns, which they had cached under their blankets, and a fight ensued in which in a few minutes' time thirty soldiers were killed and two hundred Indians, more than half of them women and children. This most deplorable affair, while directly the result of the treachery of the Indian prisoners, was in its awful fatalities attributable to the fact that the soldiers lost their heads and seeing their companions falling about them spared nothing that wore a blanket.

When Short Bull and his band of three thousand Indians, who were about to resume peaceable relations at the agency, heard from Wounded Knee, they at once turned back toward the Bad Lands, where they were joined by about as many more of the Indians who had been peaceable, so that there were from five to six thousand in his camp, which he established seventeen miles from the agency. On the next day a party of seventy of the young warriors made a sally in the direction of the

agency and at the Catholic mission, about six miles west of Pine Ridge, set fire to one of the out-buildings. They were here attacked by Colonel Forsythe, who was sent out with eight troops of cavalry to drive them away. He soon found himself surrounded by the Indians and in a perilous situation, but was relieved by Major Henry, who with four troops of cavalry and a Hotchkiss gun soon had them flying. Lieutenant Mann and one private of Colonel Forsythe's force were killed. On the 3d of January, 1891, an attack was made on Colonel Carr's troops of the Sixth Cavalry, but was handsomely repulsed. At this juncture General Miles took personal command in the field and, securing communication with the leaders, established terms of peace with them, and on January 16th they came in and camped about the agency and the trouble was at an end.

During all of this time the state militia from the Black Hills rendered effective service, under Col. Merritt H. Day, scouting along the upper Cheyenne and White rivers. Ben knew that Colonel Day was backed up by Colonel Jackson and his Tennessee Militia Volunteers but the accounts in the historical records just mention that 200 volunteers saved Colonel Day on more than one occasion. Ben studied various resources regarding the KGC and the Black Hills region. It was apparent that they employed many decoy and diversion tactics in hiding their vast wealth.

Ben concluded that the Golden Circle was actually a two-part organization. The inner circle was Knights Templar and the outer circle composed of 10,000 ex-Confederate soldiers was composed of all Scottish Rite Masons. The Knights of the Golden Circle still exists in both this country and Europe though greatly reduced in numbers. According to the enlightened it is a virtually unknown fact that the

Golden Circle between the years 1865 and 1916 procured through guerilla warfare, recovery of known

hidden treasures and secret investments of stolen wealth a vast fortune conservatively estimated at

today's value of over 3 trillion dollars. It is believed that they shut down the procurement part of the

operation in 1916 and liquidated their investments in stocks and commercial operations of many kinds,

converting them into mostly gold bullion and coin. They then concealed this vast wealth in potentially

thousands of caches throughout the U.S., Canada and Mexico. Many historians have disregarded the

vast numbers of theoretical treasure locations as fantasy but Ben was starting to draw some very real

correlations of these treasure locations as possibly being the actual federal mineral patents themselves

where gold certainly had been discovered and legally purchased from the US Government after

meeting all the federal requirements.

Confederate Code Breaker
Chapter 6

Consider these Signs & Symbols :Radiant Sun, Trees in weird shapes (disfigured), Giant rock

carvings or shapes (animals, faces), Rock piles/monuments, Crosses, Hearts, Bells, Animals,

Numbers, Dates, Priests, Pyramids, Eyes, Graffiti, Jack O' Lantern Faces, Names, Initials, JJ, Dates,

Bible Passages, 3-Toed Turkey Tracks, Blazes on trees, Odd-shaped rocks,Rocks that seem out of

place, 33, Shallow buried metal objects, Small caches, Horse, Donkey, Turtle, Birds, Snakes, Indian

Chiefs, Pointing Finger, Stone Maps, Names spelled backwards, Anagrams (scrambled words),

Phonetics, Arrows, Crosses, Window Rocks, Dagger or Knife----these are just some of the clues to be

looking for around KGC depositories.

The military operations and business activities of his great great grandfather Colonel Jackson were intriguing to say the least and Ben was trying to figure out what happened to all the gold that was removed from the giant J. The records indicated a 7500 ft tunnel called the "Black Eagle" that apparently followed a vein of gold deep into the mountains.

 Ben's grandmother had no idea how much gold her grandfather had mined or where it might be today other than possibly in a Chicago bank somewhere .

Ben was reading about the Freemasons and learning about their secret symbols and how the KGC had used many Masonic symbols in their treasure maps. He was looking at a giant J goldmine and was still in shock trying to decipher the mystery. Ben kept thinking about the Freemasons and the Knights Templar's and how they were connected. He felt that the secrecy of the societies most likely made it very difficult to ever know the whole truth but if he could just understand what their significance was in relation to his family he could at least be satisfied to an extent. The hunger inside him wanted to know more.

He sent the giant J off to Bob Brewer the KGC expert in Arkansas and Bob said that he had never seen a J quite like that although many of the KGC maps reference a lower case j as a treasure marker. This information only added more interest to the situation. Maybe the giant J stands for

Jackson and also treasure or gold. Many of the KGC masonic symbols represent gold but are also a directional pointer to another clue or marker where the gold may be buried.

Ben could not shake the idea that Cibola was in the Black Hills and the KGC had discovered it just like the movie Book Of Secrets had said but how do you prove it?

He figured that the direct relation to his cousin General Stonewall Jackson was probably somehow connected to the upper ranks of the KGC and after Stonewall's death Ben's family somehow assumed more responsibility for the Confederacy.

Ben had read an interesting story about the Confederate underground and the activities of the veterans in the post war era. Doing further research on masonic symbols he stumbled across an article describing the use of a tree carving used by the Confederate underground. The Confederates would carve an actual tree into a J shape somewhere in the yard of a home to symbolize the Confederate underground that way passers by would know if it was safe.

Ben was stunned for a moment at what he was reading. Yes, verification he said! Ben's cabin

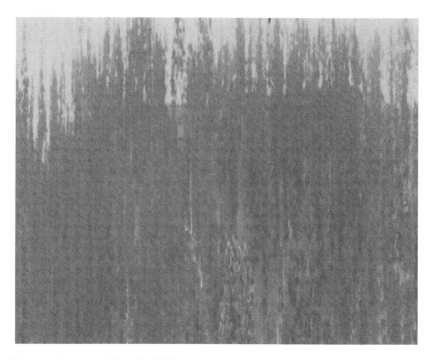

picture of Colonel Jackson,wife, and child has a J shaped tree on the hill.

Amazing! How could some article on the internet know that his cabin picture had a J shaped tree in the

yard? The J shaped tree was a small fact that Ben had noticed when examining the picture in detail

after scanning it to the computer. He figured it stood for Jackson but maybe was a treasure symbol of

some kind as well. Now he had confirmation that it meant Confederate Underground..

But where did the gold go? Ben's grandma was missing very pertinent information as to where her

grandpa Jackson had decided to put his gold.

Ben needed to really do some more heavy research to see what happened when Colonel Jackson moved back to Chicago. It appears he shut down the gold mining operation around 1910 but also had a

residence in Chicago in 1900 until 1950 when he died.

Ben began thinking about what Jack would do with a massive amount of gold. Obviously it

would have to be buried somewhere. He thought it may be in the same place that the Templar Treasure

is located and possibly the Confederate treasure. At this point in time it's probably all in the same place

regardless of who really won the civil war he speculated. Colonel Jackson is our last

known link to the Confederate treasure and it appears that he himself removed a massive amount of

gold from the giant J. The Templar Treasure might also consist of the Ark of The Covenant and the

Holy Grail.

At this point it was Ben's theory was that the KGC was somehow connected to the Masons and

the Knights Templar and somehow connected to the giant J. The masonic symbol G for God came to

mind as he thought about the masons again. He thought about Jesse James who supposedly had 72

identities. Is it possible that George Washington Jackson his 3rd great grandfather was actually Jesse

James who had stolen George's identity? Anything seemed possible when talking about Jesse James.

Ben was completely convinced that Jesse James had faked his death and was probably still in

command of the KGC well after 1882 . In order to find the treasure he would have to follow Colonel

Jackson or try and find the real Colonel Jesse Woodson James.

He said to himself it has be somewhere. The gold has got to be somewhere. Where? Underground in Chicago near grandpa Jackson's house from 1950 maybe?

Ben was familiar with the downtown Chicago area after working for his family's tour bus business in the 80's and 90's. His grandpa Jackson's home was located in the Lincoln Park/Gold Coast area of Chicago in section 33.

Right away he couldn't believe it. The masonic #33? Gold Coast? It was looking as if the Mason's had also designed the city of Chicago.

Ben had worked in the heart of the gold coast area for many years helping run his family's Double-Decker tour bus company but he never realized that his office was located in section 33.

He typed Chicago Underground into the internet and up came a link for the Chicago Tunnel Company. Ben's eyes grew wider as he read about how the company had dug 33 miles under the city of Chicago under the management of Chief Engineer George W. Jackson.

Unbelievable! Inconceivable!!

He was looking for masonic KGC treasure signs and an underground vault and sure enough he found Colonel Jackson's home located in section 33 with the name George W. Jackson connected to an elaborate underground vault system with 33 miles of tunnels. He was looking for the masonic signs and they don't get much stronger than 33.

The only other names he was looking for at this point were George W. Jackson who was Colonel Jackson's brother's name and his fathers name or he was looking for someone disguised as Jesse W. James.

Sure enough George was the next clue along with the # 33 appearing twice right where Ben was

looking for it. Amazing!

Colonel Jackson's father's name was George W. Jackson as well as one of his brothers George Jr. The Illinois Telephone and Construction Company was owned and managed by George W. Jackson who had apparently dug 16 miles under the city of Chicago without a permit or a contract to do so.

George and his underground workers apparently removed the debris spoils away covertly at night time through the back alley door of his bar located on Madison st. They dug 40 ft down to the middle of the intersection and just kept on going for 33 miles.

Ben noticed strong similarities to a typical Confederate Depository layout pointed out in "Shadow of the Sentinel" by Bob Brewer and Warren Getler.

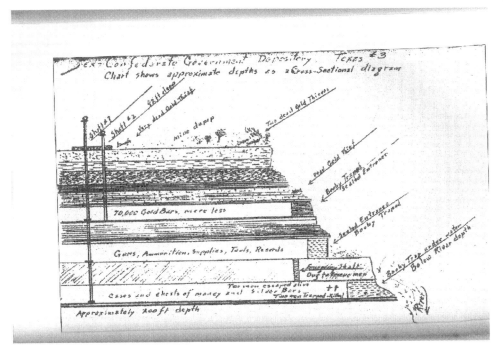

They eventually obtained a permit and a city contract to run telephone cable through the tunnels

along with freight such as coal and mail. Although, the article didn't mention gold Ben was thinking it

the whole time. They moved the tunnel operation from the bar to a warehouse still on Madison st just 2

blocks from the Federal Reserve Building. The tunnels were connected to all the federal buildings and

banks where mail and freight such as coal or even gold possibly could be shipped underground.

Ben decided it was time to go downtown and see Colonel Jackson's house in person and to scout out

the area for any obvious KGC treasure markers.

It was a beautiful summer day in 2011 as he parked the Jeep down the street and started walking

to the address on Sedgwick st. As he walked up to where the house was suppose to be it was obviously

not there anymore nor was the address. He couldn't help noticing that the letters KGC were imbedded

in the word Sedgwick. There were few things that were actually adding up to coincidence and Ben had

read how clues were also hidden in certain words such as Anagrams or scrambled words containing

masonic symbols. KGC being scrambled into Sedgwick was actually probably just a coincidence but

then he tried to think of another street with KGC hidden in the word but could not.

After talking with a man in his front lawn Ben had learned that the address was changed and the

corner buildings had been demolished to build a CVS pharmacy.

Ben decided to walk a few blocks to the Chicago Historical building and see if they had any

information on the tunnels. Ben noted several masonic symbols in the area along his walk especially

the statute of Benjamin Franklin. He took the elevator to the top floor of the historical society building

and entered the records room where a nice lady assisted him. She quickly pulled out a book by Bruce

Moffat called the Chicago Tunnel Story.

Then she pulled up micro film of Sedgwick st in the 1950's and sure enough they had changed

the address on Colonel Jackson's property which was now a real estate office with several added levels.

Ben absorbed the new information and read through the book about the Chicago tunnel system.

At this point Ben was following a Confederate Code system that had led him from Chicago to his family's giant J in the Black Hills where he has determined a direct relation to General Stonewall and General Andrew Jackson to each other and to his own family and also that his great great grandfather was the last active Colonel on US soil at the end of the Indian wars and 2nd in command to General Miles out of Chicago. Ben had about 10 minutes left before the Historical Society was closing so he had to speed read through as much of the book as possible.

5 minutes into the speed read Ben came across the information he thought he was possibly looking for but it was even more than what he expected. It said right there in the book that George W Jackson designed and constructed the 33 miles of tunnels connecting all the banks to the Federal Reserve but the book also said 2 very important things that Ben was amazed to learn and it also confirmed his theory even more. The book said that George W. Jackson was a Freemason and a Knights Templar as if these were just regular social groups like the Cub scouts or something.

Ben sat there dazed and in shock until people started packing up their supplies and heading for the exit door as the building was preparing to close.

He started walking the 5 blocks back to his car and had a feeling of incredible satisfaction but now that his theory was confirmed there were even more questions lingering.

Ben was thoroughly convinced as he drove out of the city that his family had buried a massive treasure under the city somewhere but how was he going to dig it up.

He got back to his home office and began reviewing the schematics of the tunnel system and was considering entering the tunnel system to see what clues might be underground. He quickly learned that since 9/11 the tunnels have been closed due to security risks and potential attacks from terrorists.

The intersection near Colonel Jackson's home of Sedgwick St, Armitage Ave, and Lincoln Ave are the only 3 street intersection in the city with Lincoln on a 45 angle running through Lincoln Park into the Gold coast area.

Ben could not help recognize the coded scramble of the KGC lettering written in Sedgwick and Armitage representing the military Arm of the KGC and and their obvious intersection with Lincoln for causing a northern war of aggression that had ultimately gotten Lt. General Stonewall Jackson killed regardless of whether it was an accident or an assassination. The Confederacy had been transformed into a seriously bitter agenda with the loss of their greatest General. Stonewall had been killed in action by supposed friendly fire in 1863 and still won more battles than any other General in the entire war of either side at the wars official end in 1865. All three of these streets were crossing directly over the number 33 on the map showing the section, township and range.

The masonic signs were very prevalent in the area and there was no denial. The fact that it appeared the KGC had actually designed the downtown area and gold coast of Chicago was unbelievable. Some people might say that he was stretching for a clue but the fact is that is exactly how

the Confederates coding system was used along with a completely coded alphabet that would need a secret corresponding cipher system to read a message.

This location reminded him of the supposedly authenticated KGC treasure map Solomons Temple that was in Bob Brewers book "Shadow of the Sentinel." Ben felt like he was on the Sentinels trail and that he was getting closer to the gold. Ben studied the various masonic symbols and KGC codes very seriously as he knew they were only valuable to the people who could figure them out. Bob had told Ben via email several times that without a map or location you are just wasting your time out there.

Ben confidently told Bob that he had a map and a location and maybe more than one location.

The hunt was on and Ben knew he had to find the next clue. He had just watched a documentary about how the Black Hills was the wealthiest 100 square miles on planet earth due to the mineral wealth. He was still trying to appraise his mineral rights just for personal knowledge and began reading about the history of the Black Hills and how the pioneers and the masons went west.

There is probably no other region 100 miles long and 50 miles wide that contains such a wealth

of geological and mineralogical interest as the Black Hills of South Dakota.

In the northern portion of the Black Hills gold has been the principal mineral of value but ores

of silver, lead, zinc, tungsten, and gypsum have also been produced. The importance of the gold

production has been largely due to the Homestake mine, the largest gold mine in the United States. This

mine has produced almost without interruption since 1876 and has a record of over $200,000,000

production.

Since the Black Hills were first opened to settlement in 1876 the varied mineral deposits have

excited great interest. In fact it was the discovery of gold in 1874 which caused the opening of the area,

and the resentment of the Indians over the loss of this fine hunting ground led to the Custer Massacre

on the Little Bighorn River to the northwest in Montana on June 25, 1876.

The Black Hills are situated in the extreme western part of South Dakota and extend somewhat into

northwestern Wyoming. The region is served by the Chicago, Burlington and Quincy Railroad, the

Chicago and Northwestern and a branch of the Chicago, Milwaukee and St. Paul. The region may be

reached by way of Omaha, Chicago, Minneapolis, or Denver. Several good highways now approach the

Hills and tourists visit them in increasing numbers each year. Suitable accommodations are available at many points and good roads lead to practically all of the mines and other points of mineralogical interest.

Ben was gathering detailed and general information regarding the gold found in the black hills and determined that his property was in an area known for high grade ore as well as veins running through the hills. The variety of minerals located in the hills is also quite astonishing itself.

Igneous rocks are abundant, the most important being the pre-Cambrian granite and pegmatites of the Harney Peak region and a great series of Tertiary porphyries which occur over a wide area in the northern part and form many well known masses, of which the Devil's Tower is especially well known. The variety of the exposed rocks accounts for the great number of minerals found in the region. Many others would doubtless be found only by a very careful search. .

The deposits of the Harney Peak region are the most interesting in the Black Hills from a mineralogic standpoint, but some of the deposits of the Northern Hills are not lacking in interest. A visit to the region would scarcely be complete without at least a short visit to the Homestake gold mine and the surrounding area. Perhaps the most interesting mineral, aside from the gold which is only rarely visible, is cummingtonite, a comparatively uncommon amphibole.

Cummingtonite schist is an abundant lode rock. Common minerals include arsenopyrite, pyrrhotite, chlorite and quartz.

A number of other deposits might be mentioned as well as specific occurrences of minerals. Ben began calculating the different values of various minerals on a large scale.

Ben's overall assessment is that the mineral value is to hard to determine without further exploration.

The Masons who are expert stone workers would have certainly been involved in digging the tunnels in the giant J and probably the majority of the mines listed. Other than his own documents though Ben has not been able to find anything on the giant J gold mine called the "Black Eagle".

Colonel Jesse Woodson James Revealed
Chapter 7

Some of the postwar KGC were war-hardened ex-members of William Quantrills guerrilla force

who were men on horseback and had worn star and crescent moon lapels on their pinned up brim hats

as they rode into battle in Missouri and Kansas. Still the most famous KGC operative of them all was a

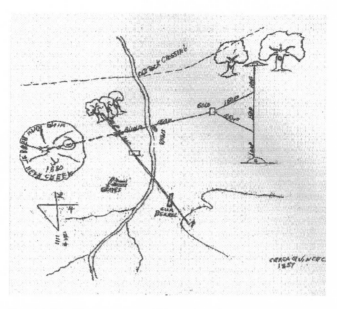

thrity-three degree Scottish Rite Freemason named Jesse Woodson James notorious for conducting

Rebel guerilla hit and run raids during the civil war and would become the KGC's master field

commander. The KGC's masterful treasure grid system employed complex cipher techniques, expert

surveyor knowledge, cryptic masonic carvings on trees and rocks, and only a limited number of coded

maps.

Ben studied an apparent authentic KGC treasure made by Jesse James and even thought he had

identified a possible location in Illinois but according to KGC expert Bob Brewer the treasure had

already been found by him and a friend in Oklahoma. Ben spent several days in the field with the map

in Northern Illinois at a spot he thought had all the right landmarks but halted the search after no luck.

The buried treasures had to be protected and watched over by Sentinels of loyal families that would dedicate their lives from generation to generation with the primary goal of guarding and being on the lookout for trespassers. It is true that Colonel James had given orders to "shoot first and ask question's later" when it came to securing the KGC hoards of gold. The shoot first order is a common trend among today's special forces commanders ironically.

Ben decided to go back to the civil war documents and try and find the KGC connection to Colonel Jackson. The Confederate veterans pension list had shown Colonel Jackson's parents as George W. Jackson and Rebecca James Jackson.

Ben was apprehensive about the next search because he just had a feeling by now that Colonel Jackson's mother and Ben's 3rd great grandmother Rebecca James Jackson was leading him directly to the real Jesse Woodson James. He stood and looked out the window of his office in deep thought. What if he was directly related to Jesse James? What if Rebecca's father was Jesse James?

Ben couldn't think straight for about 10 minutes. He went out to his garage and threw darts at his dart board while pondering such a thing. He decided to go look into the vault system and then continue with the lineage search for Jesse James.

The newly tightened security was going to make the tunnels near impossible to access and may even result with Ben ending up in jail or detained by Homeland Security or Secret Service if not careful. He began reading about the almost identical design in London that the Templar's had built and designed with the authorization from King James.

While looking at the layout of the Federal Reserve System it began to remind him of something he had seen before in the KGC records. There are 12 Reserve banks in the Federal Reserve system. According to some supposedly authentic KGC records their were 12 major depositories for the Confederate treasury representing 12 states and then one smaller 13th KGC hoard for the smallest state.

.

It was a stretch but entirely possible the Federal Reserve was actually the Confederate treasure that was making interest rather than being buried somewhere and making no interest. It doesn't really seem like very good business management practices to not have the money working for you and getting larger, much much larger. Ben had heard that the Federal Reserve was privately owned recently on various radio shows and was actually a pretty hot political subject at the moment. Nobody really has any idea who owns the Fed for sure but Ben was determined to verify as much of this as possible. The more he thought about it the more it made sense to him and he even began telling random people that he owned the Federal Reserve as a joke in random conversations.

Ben took a couple days during the summer of 2011 to recap the situation and reflect for a moment. He had spent over 2 years searching for his family's mining property which turned out to be a giant J goldmine tied to a military operation that was relatively a secret within the family.

He had verified a direct blood relation to Confederate Lt. General Thomas Jonathan "Stonewall" Jackson and to the 7th President of the United States General Andrew "Old Hickory"Jackson. He had also proven the direct relation between "Stonewall" and "Old Hickory"that historians had tried vigorously to prove for 150 years.

Ben's Jackson line clearly shows that General Andrew Jackson's grandfather was Dr. Joseph Jackson which had been the missing or unproven link. Stonewall's Great Grandfather John Jackson an immigrant from Ireland was the brother to Andrew's Grandpa Dr. Joseph Jackson.

Ben had linked the Jackson line all the way back to 1290 A.D. in England. He had linked his ancestors to the Freemasons, Knights Templar, and to the Confederate Underground.

He had most likely successfully tracked the gold from the giant J to an elaborate underground vault and tunnel system that was constructed covertly with all the signs of a federal operation similar to the giant J military operation in the Black Hills. He was thoroughly convinced that the giant J was the lost city of Cibola that they were in search of in the movie "Book of Secrets" starring Nicholas

Cage as treasure hunter Ben Gates.

They assert that if the KGC had found Cibola then the Confederates would have won the war for sure and Ben was convinced at this point that this unbelievable concept were true.

The movie's so called treasure map carved over 500 years ago had even referenced that the treasure seeker should surrender his or her hand to the noble bird and the name of the giant J goldmine was the "Black Eagle". An eagle is certainly a noble bird.

Ben had proven that J. Frank Dalton's story the self proclaimed Jesse James from the 1940' was not just a completely crazy con artist after all.

Whoever Dalton really was he certainly knew some serious KGC information because he had said that the real Jesse Woodson James was really cousins to the Jesse James of Clay County Missouri and the name Jesse Robert James never even surfaced when the KGC faked the death of Jesse Woodson James in 1882.

Ben had looked up the microfilm of the 1850 federal census for the 4 year old Jesse James and verified that the guy in Missouri was positively named Jesse R James and his father was Robert James. The 1860 census had obviously been altered with an ink pen to make the middle initial R look like a W.

This was truly amazing. Ben copied the census and sent it off to treasure hunter Bob Brewer who had already seen it before and completely agreed with Dalton's story that Jesse Woodson James had successfully faked his death in 1882 although Bob had no idea who the real Jesse Woodson James was in reality.

This news was really historically groundbreaking. Ben talked with the James Farm in Missouri that was now a museum and the expert did not know what to say about the census information showing Jesse R James. The expert asked Ben "so you are saying that the real Jesse Woodson James didn't even really live on this farm?"

Ben said yes that is correct! She then said that Robert James did have a documented brother named John W James when Ben inquired about the records on file.

Ben noted the JWJ initials and figured that Jesse was possibly another name for John W James and would be more of an accurate age profile for the Jesse Woodson James that was a civil war veteran and the most likely commander of the KGC.

The historically known birth year of Jesse Woodson James was 1847 which makes him 14 when the civil war began in 1861. We now know that his cousin Jesse Robert James was born in 1847 but we don't know when the real JWJ was born.

Ben was thinking that proving the true identity of Jesse Woodson James was the key to proving the Confederates and the KGC won the war through the banking system which ultimately led to the creation of the Federal Reserve.

If this were true it would completely rewrite history obviously for everyone. What, the south won the war? C'mon that's not what the school books say!

This would also completely change the the known history of Jesse James from being a gang member and legendary outlaw to the military Colonel of the KGC and the last active Colonel of the Confederate Army and ultimate rebel of the the civil war. This knew outlook shows Jesse Woodson James as the ultimate commander of the rebel army underground that was not robbing for his own greed and pleasure but was still every bit engaged in a war that had not yet ended in the eyes of the KGC.

Ben read that Jesse Woodson James was an expert marksman and wilderness survivalist that lived off the land while commanding an army that was politically aligned to the Knights Templar of London and most likely directly related to King James according to an obscure article that had mentioned the lineage of Jesse James that was most likely true he thought based on probability and the uniqueness of the legendary outlaw.

The image of the real Jesse James was actually starting to look more like that of 007 British

Secret Service Agent James Bond but commanding an army of KGC agents from the deep Wilderness

areas of the United States and using cryptic masonic codes to bury treasure all over the vast wilderness

areas between 1866-1890. It appears that next to Ben's cousin Stonewall, Jesse W James was the

biggest hero of the Confederate Army and won the war for the south although history has proclaimed

that there is no evidence that Jesse James ever used the money for anything but himself.

It was pretty clear that his known cousin Jesse R James in Missouri was where history has derived most

of the information about a man that seemed to be a legendary ghost.

According to Dalton, Jesse R James was also in the KGC and moved to Canada for a short time

directly after the 1882 death hoax of his cousin Jesse Woodson James.

The question is what happened to the Confederate treasure that the KGC buried? Was it left in the wilds

of the far west or did they dig it back up and secure them into the newly constructed vaults at the Fed.

Ben has linked the Jackson's and the giant J goldmine to the underground tunnel and vault

system that connects to the Federal Reserve Bank of Chicago.

Now in order to connect the Federal Reserve to Jesse James he will have to find the missing

link to his 3rd great grandmother Rebecca James Jackson. He had been putting this off because he just

thought that the surname James is very common like Jackson and the odds are highly unlikely of also being related to Jesse James along with Stonewall Jackson, Andrew Jackson, and 2 Indian chiefs.

He was still recovering from the shock of being directly related to several famous Generals and Colonels in the Jackson bloodline and now it was time to start another quest entirely. If he is right about his Jesse James theory then he can essentially set the record straight for a man and leader that had fought so unbelievable hard to preserve a future for his devoted people.

Ben logged onto his Ancestry.com account and began looking at the family tree and searching for the father of Rebecca James Jackson his 3rd great grandmother. The Jackson family tree at the county archives had her last name listed incorrectly as Howell with her father being from North Carolina. Ben checked that fact out and the 1880 census clearly shows her father's birthplace being in Tennessee. He had verified that the Confederate veterans pension list has George W. Jackson's wife listed as Rebecca James Jackson

He wondered if that was an honest mistake or if her maiden name had been deliberately changed so that people researching Jesse James in that area of Tennessee would not look there.

Ben did a couple searches in the Nashville,Tennessee area for all Rebecca's born in 1839 plus or minus 2 years. The first name that came up was Rebecca Howell in Nashville born in 1838. It was obvious that who ever did the Jackson family chart at the archives had chosen that Rebecca because it is the closest match to age and location but the second match was Rebecca James born in 1839.

This was it! The defining moment Ben has been waiting for and this search took only 10 minutes after filling in all the other blanks to get us to this point.

Ben knew this was it. This was the clincher and the moment of truth to determining if his entire grand theory was reality or just a bunch of coincidences. He thought about that old saying that there is no such thing as coincidences. He starred at the computer for a moment.

He said OK the Quest of The Giant J has led me to this point for a reason. He knew at this point in his soul that he was related to Jesse James. He could feel that the entire quest for the truth was being pushed by an invisible driving energy that was real. The powerful energy and mysterious spiritual force that he had been feeling during his entire quest was now looking right back at him clear as day.

He knew that when he clicked that button it was going to show a very real connection to the real Jesse Woodson James the same guy who had been granted access to the Black Hills and 2 wagon loads of gold by Chief Sitting Bull himself in exchange for new repeating rifles and guerilla warfare training.

The direct blood relation to the Colonel of the KGC was one click away. What will it say he asked himself as he starred at the computer screen? If it he were wrong it would say something completely off the mark like Fred James or something.

If he were right it would either say Jesse James or Frank James or someone closely related to the real

Jesse W James.

Ben clicked on the link and he just sat there in his chair starring at the computer for about 10

minutes straight. The computer said that a man named J W James was Ben's 4th great grandfather and it

was now official.

1850 United States Federal Census

Name:	**J W James**
Age:	30
Estimated Birth Year:	abt 1820
Birth Place:	Tennessee
Gender:	Male
Home in 1850 (City,County,State):	District 18, Gibson, Tennessee
Family Number:	1870
Household Members:	Name
	J W James
	Lucinda James
	Rebecca James
	George James
	William James
	Allen James
	G B Mcwhorter
	Henry Roane
	Louisa Roane
	William Parker
	Alex Mcgeehee
	Leonard Owens

Adding it to the family tree started another branch of lineage in the James line that was going to lead to another search most likely connecting to King James although that would have to wait and was not

a crucial element at the moment.

The 1850 census in Gibson county Tennessee shows that the real JWJ was 30 years old and born in

1820 and occupation is listed as a Saddler. Seems like an appropriate occupation for someone who

was always reported to have the most amazing saddle completely covered with silver inlay and master

craftsmanship.

That is an interesting thought as he began to envision Jesse James working in the barn building

beautiful custom silver saddles prior to the civil war. He was known to be an expert horseman with

a big interest of horse racing in the Nashville area. Ben also noticed that the real Jesse Woodson James

did have a son named George.

Another interesting note is that J. Frank Dalton back in the 1940's who claimed to be Jesse Woodson

James born in Kentucky 1844 said his father was Capt George James from Kentucky. The interesting

thing is that although J. Frank Dalton has been discredited as being the real JWJ he has been accredited

by KGC experts as to being correct about a number of KGC treasure depositories as well as inside

information pertaining to the James family like the fact that the Jesse James from Missouri was really

(JRJ) Jesse Robert James and cousins to the real Jesse Woodson James but that name never surfaced

when the KGC faked the death of the real Jesse Woodson James. George James shown as the son

of the real JW James was born in 1844 in Tennessee. Ben felt that this George James was

the same age and was possibly really J. Frank Dalton who was revealing only certain information for those that had the clues and family information to find the Confederate treasures that were once guarded by their KGC Sentinel ancestors like in Bob Brewers and Ben's family.

Once again you would need a map or known location to start searching for KGC clues.

The Jesse James connection in Tennessee has always been big and the KGC had their headquarters in Nashville during the civil war so it all seems more logical then living in Missouri or anywhere else although it does appear that the James family did also have relatives in Kentucky and many other places.

Rebecca was his eldest child being born when Jesse was just 19 years old in 1839.

The 1850 census for Rebecca James shows her father as a J W James and mother Lucinda. She married George Washington Jackson Ben's 3rd great grandfather who was cousins to General Stonewall Jackson. Ben knew he had just entered the inner sanctum of the KGC and proven that the real J W James who was friends with Sitting Bull most surely was not from Missouri and ultimately faked his death in 1882 and built the Federal Reserve with the assistance of General Stonewall Jackson's extended family.

Where else do you put the Confederate Treasure? Not making interest over the last 100 years would be poor management on behalf of the Jackson family.

Ben looked out the window of his suburban Chicago home which he calls Fort Apache as the

sun began to set to the west streaming through the trees when he realized he was probably going to

have to write a book to set the record straight about the real Jesse James.

Ben felt that Jesse's spirit would appreciate a correction in the historical record that never even

knew the complex reality of such a man. History was right about a few things concerning Jesse James

but far from the truth in reality.

One interesting concept that had gained Ben's attention was the fact that he had felt feelings or

memory's pertaining to Jesse James. He realized this had occurred many times in the past but obviously

didn't relate them to Jesse James. He even remembered reading an article many years ago when he was

a kid and could remember then that he felt that he might be related but could not explain why he felt

that way. Ben was talking with friend Dave Nelson at a party who mentioned the fact that do to

"Genetic Memory" elephants could remember a watering hole that an ancestor had been to but itself

had never actually been to in reality.

Ben wondered if he could possibly unconsciously know things about Jesse James or Colonel

Jackson's treasure activities from some type of Genetic Memory? The more he read it became more and

more plausible of an idea.

Genetic memory, sometimes called *ancestral memory,* is, in contrast, the genetic transmission of sophisticated knowledge itself, or at least the genetic transmission of the templates or 'rules' of such knowledge. One might refer to these as the musical chip, artistic chip, calendar-calculating chip or mathematical chip, for example.

This is not an entirely new concept. Brill, in 1940, quoted Dr. William Carpenter who, in comparing Zerah Colborn's calculating powers to Mozart's mastery of musical composition, defined these "congenital gifts" as "intuitions". He wrote: "in each of the foregoing cases, then, we have a peculiar example of the possession of an extraordinary congenital aptitude for certain mental activity, which showed itself at so early a period as to exclude the notion that it could have been acquired by the experience of the individual. To such congenital gifts we give the name of intuitions; it can scarcely be questioned that like the instincts of the lower animals, they are the expressions of constitutional tendencies embodied in the organism of the individuals who manifest them."

In a 2004 essay, Keith Chandler ascribes the savant's ability to "to remember things they never learned," to para-normal phenomena, and other writers have extended such abilities to include past life regression. My view of 'genetic memory' does not extend to, nor include those phenomenon or mechanisms. My view of 'genetic memory' is more narrow, in fact, than even Jung's "collective unconscious." It is generally accepted that we can inherit certain physical characteristics such as height, weight, hair color, eye color and even propensity to certain diseases, for example. It is also generally accepted that certain behavioral traits, or even talents, can 'run in families' and we see evidence of that all around us. Genetic memory simply adds bits of inherited *knowledge* to that passed on mix of genes, chromosomes and cells instead than settling for the view that we start our lives with completely blank memory or knowledge disks to which we add only those life experiences and learning that occur after we are born.

Ben considered for a second that this whole code breaking adventure was actually a genetic transfer of information from Jesse James and Colonel Jackson themselves. It is the only answer that would explain why Ben felt the intense desire to find the property even when nobody believed he could.

There are a lot of things people could spend their time on but for some reason Ben was determined to see this mystery through until he had no more urge to do so. Slavery was beginning to become unprofitable even by George Washington's time. In the succeeding years, Southern planters

saw themselves losing more and more of their wealth. Their nervousness over this loss of wealth

coupled with the fact that the new Republican Party (founded in 1854) wanted to end slavery altogether

without any government compensation to slave owners - was the main cause of the American Civil

War. April 12, 1861 Confederate forces under General P.G.T. Beauregard bombard Major Robert

Anderson and his Union soldiers at Fort Sumter in Charleston, South Carolina. The Civil War officially

begins. Ben has cracked the KGC codes and is hot on the trail of the Confederate treasure that

some people have spent their entire lives trying to find.

The Fed
Chapter 8

Ben had reviewed all the material and was preparing to contact the Federal Reserve about the

giant J gold reserves that Colonel Jackson had accumulated and the Confederate treasury.

It was quite obvious at this point that Colonel Jackson C. Jackson being the grandson of Colonel James

most surely knew where the Confederate treasure was located and was directly involved in

watching ofter it. There were reports from J Frank Dalton and others that Jesse's

grandson had been present at many of the KGC meetings. It could have been George W Jackson Jr who

managed the tunnel and vault construction as well. Either way it was a family affair and the inner

sanctum of the KGC was certainly one with strong southern roots that have spread to Chicago and the

western frontier.

The Fed was created in 1913 with a new building going up in 1922 on the corner of LaSalle St.

and Jackson Blvd. LaSalle was a French Explorer and affiliated Mason which Ben had noted on the way to the Chicago Historical society. It seemed LaSalle st was certainly a major street utilized in the

tunnel system based on the schematics of the tunnels.

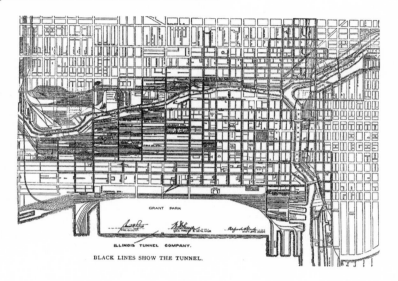

GRANT PARK

ILLINOIS TUNNEL COMPANY.
BLACK LINES SHOW THE TUNNEL.

Ben decided to call the Federal Reserve Bank in Chicago and ask them about the gold.

Surprisingly, he was patched through to a specific office after explaining the giant J goldmine situation

and his belief that his family built the Reserve system in Chicago with the gold. After calling back a

couple more times he was put in touch with a specific office where a man named Dan Masterman had

given him some advice to send in his giant J documents.

The contact at the Reserve Bank in Chicago said he should send in his giant J documents because it makes sense and would probably have to do so eventually anyway.

Ben was a bit confused at how cordial and accepting they were of his outlandish story but began

preparing his documents for the Federal Reserve bank to review essentially asking them where

Colonel Jackson's gold was currently located.

Ben sent the documents off and waited patiently for a response.

A couple days before Ben had received a call from a Special Agent Tucker from the Forest Service in

the Black Hills and was asked to stop making calls regarding the giant J. The Special Agent asked him

a series of questions and stated that an investigation was already underway. He said that he would

either be filing criminal charges against Ben for scarring people or would make a recommendation to

the US Attorney General to get the county and their 3rd party buyers off the historic family property

shaped like a giant J.

The agent asked about the military use of the property at which point Ben acknowledged that it

was a business and a military post. Ben also mentioned that he had been dealing with Rick Wilson who

was the Chief of Title Matters for the United States regarding the Jackson estate. Ben informed the

agent of the corruption involved and how Rick said the judge should be arrested for not upholding his

federal property law. Then the Supreme court of South Dakota completely removed a judge from

the bench for the first time in 121 years that was law partners with Ben's judge Delmonte. He was told to file a complaint briefing with the United States Attorney General regarding corruption at the county with a recommendation from the Chief of Title Matters Rick Wilson.

Ben ran the situation through his mind and couldn't believe that it had come this far. While waiting for a response from the Federal Agent about the giant J goldmine Ben continued working on tracking down the actual gold from the mining operation as well as the Confederate Treasure. It is apparent that most historical accounts of the KGC refer to Jesse James as being solely in command of the treasure. Ben had tracked the gold from one covert military operation in the Black Hills to another covert military operation and construction of Chicago's Tunnel System which all connects to the Chicago Gold Coast and Lincoln Park in section 33 right near Colonel Jackson's last known Chicago address.

Ben had read that 30 million barrels of reserve oil had been stored in the tunnel system under Grant Park. He noted that the Rockefeller's most likely provided the black gold in the tunnel system and he had also found out that William Rockefeller was on the board of directors for the bank that had become the holding company for the tunnel system and helped finance the second half of the system. Ben now had evidence of JP Morgan and friends along with William Rockefeller making a very large business plan with George W Jackson and family.

Ben received notice from the Federal Reserve Bank of Chicago that they had no idea what he was talking about and furthermore they do not have any gold or ownership records pertaining to the issues

he raised in his inquiry.

Ben had told his friend Carl he was 99% sure the gold was there and although he knew rejection

was a possibility he was a bit surprised when reading the letter. If the gold is not there then where the

hell is it he said to himself ? Where do I go from here he said? He realized that backtracking to the

bank that had become the holding company for the tunnel system must actually be the bank that still

has the gold and probably also owns the Federal Reserve.

Ben did some investigating into what happened to the bank which was called National City

Bank of New York. Ben found a historical outline of the bank online pretty quick which really

surprised him after only doing a single search. Apparently the bank had been started in 1812 with

another name and had changed names several times over its history. By the time George W Jackson

and family had made the investment with the bank it was considered one of the largest and most

successful banks in the country and it says right in the historical background that it was the first

contributor to the Federal Reserve Bank of New York.

It had been sold and restructured and renamed a few more times after the 1930's and in 1976 it was

finally named Citibank. The current ownership was not exactly clear but the CEO of the Rockefeller

Foundation was on the Board of Directors.

Ben visited the Citibank website and it said 200 years since 1812. Ben could not help thinking about the War of 1812 when his cousin General Andrew Jackson and the Tennessee Militia defeated the British invasion.

Ben wondered if the family had a relationship with this bank even prior to the Federal Reserve creation. Andrew was certainly heavily involved in the banking system and his biggest achievement in his own words was that he "killed the bank". A different bank of course but Andy was involved in restructuring the banking system in the 1830's during his Presidency.

Ben was now feeling 100% confident that Citibank was holding his gold. He went into the local branch location and the manager was amazed by what he was being told. He said this is amazing and told Ben to contact the corporate office because this was obviously a special account and way over his head. He also agreed that the gold would have been put in the tunnels/vaults along with the black gold from the Rockefeller's after examining the giant J and tunnel information.

Ben walked out of Citibank feeling like the manager completely agreed with his wild and far fetched story about owning Citibank and the Fed and a giant J goldmine.

He contacted the corporate office shareholders dept and was asked to email in his giant J estate information. Meanwhile, he received an email from Special Agent David Tucker who notified him about a month after their first conversation that the investigation was still moving forward and asked Ben to please be patient and still refrain from calling anymore people about the giant J until he has finished his investigation.

Ben called the shareholders dept at Citibank and asked them if they had received his giant J estate documents. They acknowledged that they were reviewing the estate and were looking for his gold. Fantastic!!

Ben was positive that they had Colonel Jackson's giant J gold and the Confederate treasure and he was also aware that Jesse James had been authorized by the Knights Templar of London to be solely in command of the entire treasure. The Knights Templar were very much an inherited right of passage for the next generation which was a tradition going back to King James in the 1500's who authorized the Knights Templar's to control the banking system in the UK.

Ben had already verified that his Jackson lineage was a long line of Knights Templar's connecting back directly to King James as well. The latest and greatest Jesse James research had suggested some type or direct blood relation between Jesse Woodson James and King James.

Normally Ben would consider that information to be very questionable but now that he had the Jackson's connected back to King James it was looking like it was possibly true or at least a true political relationship was suspected most likely referring to the Knights Templar.

Just the fact that his great great grandpa Colonel Jackson was cousins to General Stonewall and

Andrew Jackson and the grandson to Colonel Jesse Woodson James was already completely

unbelievable. Now King James is involved. Even Ben could barely believe it so why would anybody

else believe his wild fairy tale.

Not to mention Chief Victorio of the Chiricahua Apache had already been verified as either being his

3rd great grandfather or a close family friend. Ben had spoken with a current Chiricahua Apache Chief

who was also ironically a Federal investigator on Indian Reservation's in the Southwest.

The Apache Chief told Ben that the tribe had verified him as being related to either Chief Victorio or

Victor Montoya who was part of Chief Victorio's band.

Ben was also invited to a few ceremonies in New Mexico over the years but do to a hectic

schedule he was unable to attend. Ben told the Chief maybe when he gets his RV he would stop on by

and say hello. Travel seemed to be on the list of things to do when he finally acquired the gold or

goldmine or both. The Grand Canyon, The Redwood trees, looking for Sasquatch, and lost pirate

treasure were all on the list of his future potential adventures.

The theft of private mineral rights nation wide now appears to be a recognized problem by federal law enforcement. The question is will they arrest Ben for telling people they are trespassing on his land or will the Feds make the county fix the situation by getting their illegal chain voided out and removed from the books. As it sits currently Ben is the trespasser and the county District Attorney doesn't care whose property they sold illegally. Sue the county in civil court is his response.

So much for serving to protect the people. Apparently all he's trying to protect is the county's bottom line. Ben's bottom line is that they are trespassing when they assess taxes on private property located in exclusive federal jurisdiction. Oop's! Look's like the counties didn't realize that many of these mineral properties issued 100 years ago have federal laws in the patents reserving legislative authority to Congress.

Ben had been over this 1000 times and those laws in the patents were conditions and stipulations of sale. Federal conditions and stipulations of sale which are specific to the newly granted owners property rights back in 1895.

Congress didn't intend property taxes for a mining operation in the middle of freakin nowhere and that is why it says in stipulation # 6 In the absence of necessary legislation by Congress the state or territory can make rules for the premises regarding easements, drainage, yatta yatta .

In the absence of necessary legislation by Congress? Meaning only when Congress is absent is the only time the that state of South Dakota or Montana or wherever have any authority to make any rules, period.

These conditions and stipulations were written under the 1866 authority forward until the early 1900's following the civil war reconstruction.

Civil war was certainly on the minds of Congress 100 years ago and a corrupt government stealing peoples mineral rights could certainly put it on the minds of many today.

In fact there were several articles and blogs going around the internet at this time all mentioning a theft of liberties and constitutional rights of many kinds.

Ben had no way of knowing that the giant J goldmine would lead to the Confederate Treasure and the Federal Reserve. That appears to be the groundwork for a great novel or fairy tale fiction story but this was Ben Miller's real life. He mentioned to Rick Wilson the Chief of Title Matters for the US that this whole corruption scandal has him feeling like he's entered the twilight zone. Now it feels as if it has shifted to an old western mixed with a tinge of James Bond 007.

Ben's friend Carl had sent him a video to check out and said it would be interesting. Ben could not believe what he was watching and 16 minutes in to the video he was just stunned. The video was a complete chronological biography of the banking empire leading up to the federal reserve called the True History of the Banking Cartels and the Federal Reserve.

In Ben's perspective it validated every thing he was saying and much more. It's accuracy was shocking even going back to the Knights Templar's and the killing of Lincoln and JFK.

Most people knew the KGC was behind Lincoln's death but Kennedy was 100 years later and was probably connected to the money again. Lincoln started his own currency as well as pushed the civil war and Kennedy threatened to kill the Fed. They both ended up dead due to pissing off some powerful bankers most likely connected to the KGC Templars.

The video even mentioned the bank that Ben had connected the treasure to which was the National City Bank of New York which later became Citibank. It showed a picture of the National City Bank of New York and a then a new Citibank location and and it's large logo on the screen.

The video explains the creation of the Fed but with no mention of the Confederate treasure or the Jackson family or Jesse James. The JP Morgans and Rockefellers are listed on the board of director records but the Jackson's appear to disappear from history after covertly building the tunnel system.

Ben was looking at the layout of the tunnel system and drew a strong similarity between the gold coast area of Chicago and Lincoln Park to the design of a KGC Template called Solomon's Temple which was supposedly an authentic KGC treasure map that Ben found in "Shadow of the Sentinel" by Bob Brewer & Warren Getler.

It was essentially a square on a 45 degree angle inside a circle with intersecting lines at all angles of a 360 degree circle . To enter Solomon' Temple the secret workman were to by all means enter from the south and commence their way northwest. When laying the Solomon template on top of the Chicago gold coast topographical map you could see how the masonic number 33 was magically aligned to the center. Three streets intersected at the 33 and was the only place in the downtown area that did so which also seemed to fit the KGC layout.

Those 3 streets at the intersection of Armitage Ave, Sedgwick St, and Lincoln Ave all cross through the number 33 on the topographical map. Ben could not help but notice the KGC and masonic symbolism all over the place. Armitage represented the heritage Arm of the Stonewall Jackson Brigade and the street Sedgwick was basically a scrambled anagram word hiding the KGC, and of course Lincoln who was killed by the Army of the KGC.

Ben also found evidence that the gold coast was once a Confederate cemetery and the old topographical map clearly had Rebel Graves marked. Ben was looking for any evidence that the Confederates had broken ground in Chicago to bury the treasure but that was before he found the tunnel system. The Sons of Confederate Veterans dug up the Gold Coast graves in 1896 apparently and moved them to a suburban cemetery because a re-design of the lakefront was being implemented.

Ben put another call into Citibank and was told that the Jackson estate is being reviewed. The days passed and Ben continued work on his newest song writing compositions. He had still not heard anything back form the Special Agent in Rapid City but was hoping to get access to his family property in the near future just like the last 2 years.

Ben looked at the KGC map of Solomon's Temple and realized that the reference of Solomon is not insignificant and is essentially connecting the Confederate Treasure to the Templar treasure in this elaborate underground tunnel banking system.

As Ben looked through all the material he had a very interesting idea. The photo of the fort with Colonel Jackson just might also have Jesse James in the picture. How absolutely amazing!

Ben has looked at the photo a million times but never considered that Jesse W James might be an old man by the time it was taken in 1901.

Ben contacted Bob Schmitt a facial recognition expert who worked on a Jesse James History show to see if he could authenticate the photo of the Fort with Colonel Jackson and possibly an older Jesse James after his supposed death in 1882.

Bob says with 96% accuracy the software can tell one way or the other if its the same guy.

Ben noticed that the oldest guy in the photo out of eleven is the only guy that could be Jesse W James based on the new age profile he has discovered.

The fort picture is from 1901 and Jesse W James born in 1820 would be 81 years old. Still time left to build the Fed in his 90's as well with his grandsons who were also Colonels and Knights Templar's.

Ben figured it was worth trying to authenticate because it could make the picture worth much more.

Ben sent the photos off to Bob Schmitt and he tried to match the old man in the photo to known Jesse James photos. Maybe the Fort Lookout photo will identify Jesse W James once and for all.

Ben looked at the possibility that the KGC left other treasures or payroll caches out there in the vast wilderness. Bob Brewer is considered a KGC expert and has found over $200,000 in KGC payroll coins buried in various KGC locations.

Ben concluded that based on his information there is quite possibly more treasure to be found but agreed with Bob that you would either need a map or location and even then you need to find the treasure which may or may not still exist.

Ben was confident that the tunnel system and Fed were created to house the majority of the treasure and even the Branch Manager at Citibank looked at the documents and said yes I agree, the tunnels were built to store the gold.

The Citibank shareholders office listened to his story and said that it was ridiculous to go into a local branch because this would obviously be a special account.

The
Knights Templar
Chapter 9

Ben began finely tuning his guitar as well as his research on the KGC connection to the Knights Templar. He made a call to the Archdiocese Catholic Church in Chicago and was told by the Cardinals assistant that the Knights Templar was not real anymore and was just a novelty group. Ben was surprised to hear such a strong comment and firm belief that the Knights Templar didn't exist anymore.

How could she be so positive?

The government and judicial systems in the United States of America at both federal and local state levels is owned by the "Temple Crown," which is a private power. Before jumping to conclusions about the Queen of England or the Royal Families of the UK controlling the world, Ben first realized this is a different "Temple Crown". Ben's compiled research was specifically pointing to the established Templar Church, known for centuries by the world as the "Crown" or "Temple Crown" or

"Crown Templar" or "Templar Crown". Ben is seeing the multiple applications for the word Crown as the Crown Temple or Crown Templar or Templar Crown, all four being synonymous and politically connected to various kingdoms and rulers of countries from around the world.

Ben read that the Temple Church was built by the Knights Templar in two parts called the Round and the Chancel. The Round Church was consecrated in 1185 and modeled after the round Church of the Holy Sepulcher in Jerusalem. The Chancel was built in 1240 and The Temple Church serves both the Inner and Middle Temples and is located between Fleet Street and Victoria Embankment at the Thames River. Its grounds also house the Crown Offices at Crown Office Row and this Temple "Church" is outside any Canonical jurisdiction. The Master of the Temple is appointed and takes his place by sealed patent, without induction or institution. Ben was drawing immediate correlations and similarities from the Templar inner Temple design to that of the KGC 's inner sanctum.

According to many legal researchers the licensed Bar Attorneys in the U.S. owe their allegiance and give their solemn oath in pledge to the Crown Temple whether they were realizing this or not. This is simply due to the fact that all Bar Associations throughout the world are signatories and franchises to the international Bar Association located at the Inns of Court at Crown Temple, which are physically located at Chancery Lane behind Fleet Street in London. Although they vehemently deny it, all Bar

Associations in the U.S., such as the American Bar Association, the Florida Bar, or California Bar Association, are essentially franchises to the "Crown". The KGC had managed to establish their own sovereign relationship with the Templar's and essentially created the Federal Reserve which was ultimately the central banking system that that the Templar's wanted to create prior to the civil war ever beginning.

The Inns of Court to the Crown Temple use the Banking and Judicial system of the City of London which is a sovereign and independent territory and is not a part of the UK similar to Washington DC not being a part of the north American states nor is it a state.

The Queen of England is not the "Crown," as we have all been led to believe and it is rather the Bankers and Attorneys who are the actual Crown or Crown Temple. The Monarch aristocrats of England have not been ruling sovereigns since the reign of King John, circa 1215. All royal sovereignty of the old British Crown since that time has passed to the Crown Temple in Chancery.

The U.S.A. is controlled and manipulated by this private foreign power and our unlawful Federal U.S. Government is their pawn broker. The bankers and Bar Attorneys in the U.S.A. are a franchise in oath and allegiance to the Crown at Chancery, the Crown Temple Church and its Chancel located at Chancery Lane which is a manipulative body of elite bankers and attorneys from the independent City of London . The banks Rule the Temple Church and the Attorneys carry out their

Orders by controlling their victim's judiciary.

Since the first Chancel of the Temple Church was built by the Knights Templar it's easy to see that this is not a new ruling system by any means. The Chancel, or Chancery, of the Crown Inner Temple Court was where King John was located in January 1215 when the English barons demanded that he confirm

the rights enshrined in the Magna Carta. This City of London Temple was the headquarters of the Templar Knights in the UK where Order and Rule were first made, which became known as Code.

Remember all these terms, such as Crown, Temple, Templar, Knight, Chancel, Chancery, Court, Code, Order and Rule as we tie together their origins with the present American Temple Bar system.

Ben thought about his Jackson bloodline connecting back to John Jackson in 1290 in England and how the long history of Templar Codes have been used in the family.

By what authority has the "Crown" stomped on the natural sovereignty of the American people one article asks?

Is it acceptable that the U.S. Supreme Court decides constitutional issues in the U.S.A?

How can it be considered in any manner as being "constitutional" when this same Supreme Court is appointed by and not elected remind you and paid by the Federal U.S. Government?

It appears the land called North America belongs to the Crown Temple.

Ben begins to think about his giant J goldmine and wonders if the Templar's are going to assist with the situation. It appears that Citibank is the Templar bank that helped design the Fed with Colonel Jackson's authorization and funds from the Confederate treasure. Still waiting to hear from Citibank and its been about 1 month since the giant J estate documents have been sent in for review.

The legal system (judiciary) of the U.S.A. is controlled by the Crown Temple from the independent and sovereign City of London. The private Federal Reserve System, which issues fiat U.S. Federal Reserve Notes, is financially owned and controlled by the Crown from Switzerland, the home and legal origin for the charters of the United Nations, the International Monetary Fund, the World Trade Organization, and most importantly, the Bank of International Settlements. Even Hitler respected his Crown bankers by not bombing Switzerland. The Bank of International Settlements in Basel, Switzerland controls all the central banks of the G7 nations. He who controls the gold rules the world.

Ben finds a timeline similar to the video he had watched about the true story of the Federal Reserve and he concludes that the Templars of London and the Jackson Templars had obviously had an on going dispute over the banking system since the days of his cousin President Andrew Jackson. Ben reviews a number of sources and concludes that the names like the Rothschilds and JP Morgan and friends or whoever are really just other names for the Knights Templar.

It was obvious that the authority of the banking system in America came from the Knights Templar in the USA who were still fighting for financial independence from the UK Templars even though the wars had long been fought and won so we thought. Well then the London Templars devised a plan to create a Civil War which would ultimately lead to their long awaited central banking system. They pushed to get Lincoln elected to infuriate the south and cause division of the states.

The KGC oriented Knights Templars were required to make the plan come to fruition by guiding the Confederate Army underground and continuing the financail war in the post war era until they finally succeeded with creating the Federal Reserve.

The thing most people don't realize is that the souh won the war because Colonel Jesse Woodson James and Colonel "Tennesse Jack" Jackson and Colonel George W. Jackson were the ones who authorized and funded the construction of the Fed and commanded the KGC.

Most people don't think about the Jackson family in American politics after General Stonewall died and that is becuase the KGC was a very secret cabinet of the Confederate Army and Stonewalls cousin Colonel Jackson was still in active command of the Stonewall Jackson Brigade after the civil war supposedly ended. Just in case Stonewall was possibly assasinated they were not taking anymore security risks whether it be friendly fire or not. To understand the financial aspect of the Civil War Ben began tracking the history of currency and devising a timeline from the medival times of the Knights

Templar's in present day.

1823: The Rothschild s take over the financial operations of the Catholic Church, worldwide.

1827: Sir Walter Scott publishes his nine volume set, The life of Napoleon and in volume two

he states that the French Revolution was planned by the Illuminati (Adam Weishaupt) and

was financed by the money changers of Europe (The Rothschild s).

1832: President Andrew Jackson (the 7th President of the United States from 1829 to 1837),

runs the campaign for his second term in office under the slogan, "Jackson And No Bank!"

This is in reference to his plan to take the control of the American money system to benefit the

American people, not for the profiteering of the Rothschild's.

1833: President Andrew Jackson starts removing the government's deposits from the

Rothschild controlled, Second Bank of the United States and instead deposits them into banks

directed by democratic bankers.

This causes the Rothschild s to panic and so they do what they do best, contract the money

supply causing a depression. President Jackson knows what they are up to and later states,

"You are a den of thieves vipers, and I intend to rout you out, and by the Eternal God, I will rout you out."

1834: The Italian revolutionary leader, Guiseppe Mazzini, is selected by the Illuminati to direct their revolutionary program throughout the world and would serve in that capacity until he died in 1872.

1835: On January 30, an assassin tries to shoot President Jackson, but miraculously both of

the assassin's pistols misfired. President Jackson would later claim that he knew the

Rothschild s were responsible for that attempted assassination. He is not the only one, the

assassin, Richard Lawrence, who was found not guilty by reason of insanity, later bragged that

powerful people in Europe had hired him and promised to protect him if he were caught.

The Rothschild s acquire the rights in the Almadén quicksilver mines in Spain. This was at the

time the biggest concession in the world and as quicksilver was a vital component in the

refining of gold or silver this gave the Rothschild s a virtual world monopoly.

1836: Following his years of fighting against the Rothschild s and their central bank in

America, President Andrew Jackson finally succeeds in throwing the Rothschild s central bank

out of America, when the bank's charter is not renewed. It would not be until 1913 that the

Rothschild s would be able to set up their third central bank in America, the Federal Reserve, and to ensure no mistakes are made, this time they will put one of their own bloodline, Jacob Schiff, in charge of the project.

Nathan Mayer Rothschild dies and the control of his bank, N. M. Rothschild & Sons is passed on to his younger brother, James Mayer Rothschild.

1837: The Rothschild s send one of their own, August Belmont, an Ashkenazi Jew, to America to salvage their banking interests defeated by President Andrew Jackson.

1840: The Rothschild s become the Bank of England's bullion brokers. They set up agencies in California and Australia.

1841: President John Tyler (the 10th President of the United States From 1841 to 1845) vetoed the act to renew the charter for the Bank of the United States. He goes on to receive hundreds of letters threatening him with assassination.

1844: Salomon Mayer Rothschild purchases the United Coal Mines of Vítkovice and Austro-Hungarian Blast Furnace Company that would go on to be one of the top ten global industrial concerns.

Benjamin Disraeli, an Ashkenazi Jew (who would go on to become British Prime Minister twice - the only admitted Ashkenazi Jew to do so) publishes Coningsby, in which he characterizes Nathan Mayer Rothschild as,

"the Lord and Master of the money markets of the world, and of course virtually Lord and Master of everything else. He literally held the revenues of Southern Italy in pawn, and Monarchs and Ministers of all countries courted his advice and were guided by his suggestions."

1845: The Great American Patriot, Andrew Jackson (7th President of the United States) dies. Before his death he is asked what he regarded his as greatest achievement. He replies without hesitation,

"I Killed The Bank,"

This is in reference to the fact he banished the Rothschild s Second Bank of the United States in 1836.

Jacob (James) Mayer Rothschild (who by now had married his niece, Betty, Salomon Mayer Rothschild's daughter), now known as Baron James de Rothschild, wins the contract to build the first major railway line across the country.

This was called the Chemin De Fer Du Nord and ran initially from Paris to Valenciennes and then joined with the Austrian rail network built by his brother (and wife's father - all sounds a bit sordid doesn't it) Salomon Mayer Rothschild.

1847: Lionel De Rothschild now married to the daughter of his uncle, Kalmann (Carl) Mayer

Rothschild, is elected to the parliamentary seat for the City of London.

A requirement for entering parliament was to take an oath in the true faith of a Christian.

Lionel De Rothschild refused to do this as he was Jewish and his seat in parliament remained

empty for 11 years until new oaths were allowed. He must have been an invaluable

representative for his constituency, bearing in mind he could never vote on any bill as he

never entered parliament.

1848: Karl Marx, an Ashkenazi Jew, publishes, "The Communist Manifesto."Interestingly at

the same time as he is working on this, Karl Ritter of Frankfurt University was writing the

antithesis which would form the basis for Freidrich Wilhelm Nietzsche's, "Nietzscheanism."

This Nietzecheanism was later developed into Fascism and then into Nazism and was used to

forment the first and second world wars.

Marx, Ritter, and Nietzsche were all funded and under the instruction of the Rothschild s. The

idea was that those who direct the overall conspiracy could use the differences in those two so-

called ideologies to enable them to divide larger and larger factions of the human race into

opposing camps so that they could be armed and then brainwashed into fighting and destroying each other, and particularly, to destroy all political and religious institutions. The same plan put forward by Weishaupt in 1776.

Eva Hanau, Amschel Mayer Rothschild's wife dies.

1849: Gutle Schnaper, Mayer Amschel Rothschild's wife dies. Before her death she would nonchalantly state,

"If my sons did not want wars, there would be none."

1850: Construction begins this decade on the manor houses of Mentmore in England and Ferrières in France, more Rothschild s Manors will follow throughout the world, all of them filled with works of art.

Jacob (James) Rothschild in France is said to be worth 600 million francs, which at the time was 150 million francs more than all the other bankers in France put together.

1852: N.M. Rothschild & Sons begins refining gold and silver for the Royal Mint and the Bank of England and other international customers.

1853: Nathaniel de Rothschild, the son in law of Jacob (James) Mayer Rothschild, purchases Château Brane Mouton, the Bordeaux vineyard of Mouton, and renames it Château Mouton Rothschild.

1854: Caroline Stern, Salomon Mayer Rothschild's wife, dies.

1855: Amschel Mayer Rothschild dies.

Salomon Mayer Rothschild dies.

Kalmann (Carl) Mayer Rothschild dies.

1858: Lionel De Rothschild finally takes his seat in parliament when the requirement to take an oath in the true faith of a Christian is broadened to include other oaths. He becomes the first Jewish member of the British parliament.

1861: President Abraham Lincoln (16th President of the United States from 1860 till his assassination in 1865) approaches the big banks in New York to try to obtain loans to support the ongoing American civil war. As these large banks were heavily under the influence of the Rothschild s, they offer him a deal they know he cannot accept, 24% to 36% interest on all monies loaned.

Lincoln is very angry about this high level of interest and so he prints his own debt free money and informs the public that this is now legal tender for both public and private debts.

1862: By April $449,338,902 worth of Lincoln's debt free money has been printed and distributed. He states of this,

"We gave the people of this republic the greatest blessing they ever had, their own paper money to pay their own debts."

That same year The Times of London publishes a story containing the following statement,

"If that mischievous financial policy, which had its origin in the North American Republic, should become integrated down to a fixture, then that government will furnish its own money without cost. It will pay off debts and be without a debt. It will have all the money necessary to carry on its commerce.

It will become prosperous beyond precedent in the history of civilized governments of the world. The brains and the wealth of all countries will go to North America. That government must be destroyed or it will destroy every monarchy on the globe."

1863: President Abraham Lincoln discovers the Tsar of Russia, Alexander II (1855 – 1881), was having problems with the Rothschild s as well as he was refusing their continual attempts to set up a central bank in Russia. The Tsar then gives President Lincoln some unexpected help.

The Tsar issued orders that if either England or France actively intervened in the American Civil War, and help the South, Russia would consider such action a declaration of war, and take the side of President Lincoln. To show that he wasn't messing about, he sent part of his

Pacific Fleet to port in San Francisco and another part to New York.

The Rothschild banking house in Naples, Italy, C. M. de Rothschild e figli, closes following the

unification of Italy. The Rothschild s use one of their own in America, John D. Rockefeller, to

form an oil business called Standard Oil which eventually takes over all of its competition.

1864: Rothschild, August Belmont, who by now is the Democratic Party's National Chairman,

supports General George McClellan as the Democratic nominee to run against President

Abraham Lincoln in this year's election. Much to the anger of Belmont, President Lincoln

wins the election.

1865: In a statement to Congress, President Abraham Lincoln states,

"I have two great enemies, the Southern Army in front of me, and the financial institutions in

the rear. Of the two, the one in my rear is my greatest foe."

Later that year, on April 14, President Lincoln is assassinated, less than two months before the

end of the American Civil War.

Following a brief training period in the Rothschild s London Bank, Jacob Schiff, a Rothschild, born in their house in Frankfurt, arrives in America at the age of 18, with instructions and the

finance necessary to buy into a banking house there. The purpose of this was to carry out the

following tasks.

Gain control of America's money system through the establishment of a central bank.

Find desirable men, who for a price, would be willing to serve as stooges for the Illuminati and promote them into high places in the federal government, the Congress, Supreme Court, and all the federal agencies.

Create minority group strife throughout the nations, particularly targeting the whites and blacks.

Create a movement to destroy religion in the United States, with Christianity as the main target.

Nathaniel de Rothschild becomes Member of Parliament for Aylesbury in Buckinghamshire.

1868: Jacob (James) Mayer Rothschild dies, shortly after purchasing Château Lafite, one of

the four great premier grand cru estates of France. He is the last of Mayer Amschel

Rothschild's sons to die.

1870: Nathaniel de Rothschild dies.

1871: An American General named, Albert Pike, who had been enticed into the Illuminati by

Guissepe Mazzini, completes his military blueprint for three world wars and various revolutions throughout the world, culminating into moving this great conspiracy into its final

stage.

The first world war is to be fought for the purpose of destroying the Tsar in Russia,as

promised by Nathan Mayer Rothschild in 1815. The Tsar is to be replaced with communism

which is to be used to attack religions, predominantly Christianity. The differences between

the British and German empires are to be used to forment this war.

The second world war is to be used to forment the controversy between fascism and political

Zionism with the slaughter of Jews in Germany a lynchpin in bringing hatred against the

German people. This is designed to destroy fascism (which the Rothschild s created) and

increase the power of political Zionism. This war is also designed to increase the power of

communism to the level that it equaled that of united Christendom.

The third world war is to be played out by stirring up hatred of the Muslim world for the

purposes of playing the Islamic world and the political Zionists off against

one another. Whilst this is going on, the remaining nations would be forced to fight

themselves into a state of mental, physical, spiritual and economic exhaustion.

On August 15th of this year, Albert Pike writes a letter (now cataloged in the British

Museum) to Guiseppe Mazzini in which he states the following,

"We shall unleash the nihilists and the atheists and we shall provoke a great social cataclysm which in all its horror will show clearly to all nations the effect of absolute atheism; the origins of savagery and of most bloody turmoil. Then everywhere, the people will be forced to defend themselves against the world minority of the world revolutionaries and will exterminate those destroyers of civilization and the multitudes disillusioned with Christianity whose spirits will be from that moment without direction and leadership and anxious for an ideal, but without knowledge where to send its adoration, will receive the true light through the universal manifestation of the pure doctrine of Lucifer brought finally out into public view.

A manifestation which will result from a general reactionary movement which will follow the destruction of Christianity and Atheism; both conquered and exterminated at the same time."

Pike, who having been elected as Sovereign Grand Commander of the Scottish Rite of Freemasonry's Southern Jurisdiction in 1859, was the most powerful Freemason in America. He would retain that post for 32 years until his death in 1891. He also published a book on the subject in 1872 entitled, "Morals and Dogma of the Ancient and Accepted Scottish Rite of

Freemasonry," in which he candidly states the following,

"LUCIFER, the Light-bearer! Strange and mysterious name to give to the Spirit of Darkness!

Lucifer, the Son of the Morning! Is it he who bears the Light, and with its splendors

intolerable blinds feeble, sensual or selfish Souls? Doubt it not!"

1872: Prior to Giuseppe Mazzini's death this year, he makes another revolutionary leader

named Adrian Lemme his successor. Lemmy will be subsequently succeeded by Lenin and

Trotsky, then by Stalin. The revolutionary activities of all these men are financed by the

Rothschild s

1873: The loss making Rio Tinto copper mines in Spain, are purchased by a group of foreign

financiers including the Rothschild s These mines represented Europe's largest source of

copper.

1875: On January 1 of this year Jacob Schiff, now Solomon Loeb's son-in-law after marrying

his daughter, Teresa, takes control of the banking house, Kuhn, Loeb & Co. He goes on to

finance John D. Rockefeller's Standard Oil Company, Edward R. Harriman's Railroad Empire,

and Andrew Carnegie's Steel Empire. This is all with Rothschild/Knight's Templar money.

He then identifies the other largest bankers in America at that time. They are, J.P. Morgan who controls Wall Street, and the Drexels and the Biddles of Philadelphia. All the other financiers, big and little, danced to the music of those three houses. Schiff then gets the European Rothschild s to set up European branches of these three large banks on the understanding that Schiff, and therefore Rothschild, is to be the boss of banking in New York and therefore America.

N M Rothschild & Sons undertake a share issue to raise capital for the first channel tunnel project to link France to England, with half of its capital coming from the Rothschild owned Compagnie du Chemin de Fer du Nord.

This year Lionel De Rothschild also loans Prime Minister Benjamin Disraeli the finance for the British government to purchase the shares in the Suez Canal, from Khedive Said of Egypt. This was done as the Rothschild s needed this access route to be held by a government they controlled, so they could use that government's military to protect their huge business interests in the Middle East.

1876: Otto von Bismarck states,

"The division of the United States into two federations of equal force was decided long before the civil war by the high financial power of Europe. These bankers were afraid that the United States, if they remained as one nation they would most likely attain economical and financial independence which would upset their financial domination over the world.

The voice of the Rothschild s predominated and they foresaw the tremendous booty if they could substitute two feeble democracies, indebted to the financiers, to the vigorous Republic, confident and self-providing.

Therefore they started their emissaries in order to exploit the question of slavery and thus dig an abyss between the two parts of the Republic."

1879: Lionel de Rothschild dies.

1880: Rothschild agents begin formenting a series of pogroms predominantly in Russia, but also in Poland, Bulgaria and Romania. These pogroms resulted in the slaughter of thousands of innocent Jews, causing approximately 2 million to flee, mainly to New York, but also to Chicago, Philadelphia, Boston and Los Angeles.

The reason these pogroms were initiated, was to create a large Jewish base in America, who when they arrived, would be educated to register as Democrat voters. Some twenty years later, this would result in in a massive Democratic power base in the United States and be used to elect Rothschild front men such as Woodrow Wilson, to the Presidency, to carry out

the bidding of the Rothschild s

1881: President James A. Garfield (The 20th President of the United States who lasted only

100 Days) states two weeks before he is assassinated,

"Whoever controls the volume of money in our country is absolute master of all industry and

commerce...and when you realize that the entire system is very easily controlled, one way or

another, by a few powerful men at the top, you will not have to be told how periods of inflation

and depression originate."

Edmond James de Rothschild has a son Maurice de Rothschild.

1883: After 6,000 feet of tunnel in the channel tunnel project being excavated, the British

government halt the project citing the fact that it would be a threat to Britain's security.

1885: Nathaniel Rothschild, son of Lionel De Rothschild, becomes the first Jewish peer and is

takes the title of Lord Rothschild.

1886: The French Rothschild bank, de Rothschild Frères obtains substantial amounts of

Russia's oil fields and forms the Caspian and Black Sea Petroleum Company, which quickly

becomes the world's second largest oil producer.

1887: Opium trafficker in China, Edward Albert Sassoon, marries Aline Caroline de

Rothschild, the grand-daughter of Jacob (James) Mayer Rothschild. Aline Caroline's father,

Gustave, together with his brother, Alphonse, took over the Rothschild's french arm following

their father Jacob's death.

The Rothschild s finance the amalgamation of the Kimberley diamond mines in South Africa.

They subsequently become the biggest shareholders of this company, De Beers, and mine

precious stones in Africa and India.

1888: Noémie Halphen, future wife of Maurice de Rothschild born.

1891: The British Labour Leader makes the following statement on the subject of the

Rothschild s,

"This blood-sucking crew has been the cause of untold mischief and misery in Europe during

the present century, and has piled up its prodigious wealth chiefly through fomenting wars

between States which ought never to have quarreled.

Whenever there is trouble in Europe, wherever rumors of war circulate and men's minds are

distraught with fear of change and calamity you may be sure that a hook-nosed Rothschild is at his games somewhere near the region of the disturbance."

Comments like this worry the Rothschild s and towards the end of the 1800's they

purchase Reuters news agency so they can have some control of the media.

1895: Edmond James de Rothschild the youngest son of Jacob (James) Mayer Rothschild

visits Palestine and subsequently supplies the funds to found the first Jewish colonies there,

this is to further their long term objective of creating a Rothschild owned country.

1897: The Rothschild s found the Zionist Congress to promote Zionism (a political movement

with the sole aim of moving all Jews into a singularly Jewish nation state) and arrange its first

meeting in Munich. However due to extreme opposition from local Jews, who are quite happy

where they are, this meeting has to be moved to Basle, Switzerland and takes place on 29

August. The meeting is chaired by Ashkenazi Jew, Theodor Herzl, who would state in his

diaries,

"It is essential that the sufferings of Jews....become worse....this will assist in realization of our

plans....I have an excellent idea....I shall induce anti-Semites to liquidate Jewish wealth....The

anti-Semites will assist us thereby in that they will strengthen the persecution and oppression

of Jews. The anti-Semites shall be our best friends."

Herzl is subsequently elected President of the Zionist Organization which adopts the,

"Rothschild Red Hexagram or Sign," as the Zionist flag which 51 years later will end up as the

flag of Israel.

Edward Henry Harriman becomes a director of the Union Pacific Railroad and goes on to take

control of the Southern Pacific Railroad. This is all financed by the Rothschild s

1898: Ferdinand de Rothschild dies.

1895: Colonel Jackson's Brigade and the KGC acquire Cibola and add to the coffers of the Confederate

Underground.

1900: Colonel Jackson and family begin a covert operation building the Chicago Tunnel system to
store the Confederate treasure and gold from Cibola.

1913: Colonel Jackson and Colonel Jesse W James create the Federal Reserve with the National City

Bank Of New York and the Knights Templar of London. A 99 year contract/partnership is negotiated

essentially making the central bank in the UK and the Fed in the USA political and financial allies for

the next century resulting in a century of peace between the 2 nations.

1914: World War 1 Begins

A new world order is created and printed as fact "Novus Ordo Seclorum" on American

currency pro-claiming "In God We Trust" which is the typical Knights Templar

moniker.

2012: Ben Miller shows up at Citibank and and asks about a "Special Account"

2013: ?

Ben was still waiting to hear back from Special Agent Tucker in the Black Hills when noticing a

similarity to Chief Victorio and Jesse James. They both had rumors of apparently faking their death

with Victorio in 1880 and Jesse Woodson James in 1882. Ben had already proven the truth about Jesse

W James real identity and that he faked his death in 1882 but what would be the odds of being related

to 2 different famous people who possibly faked their deaths. It is a strange coincidence so Ben looked

for any possible evidence connecting Jesse James to Chief Victorio and there is a rumor that the

Mexican Emperor Maximilian

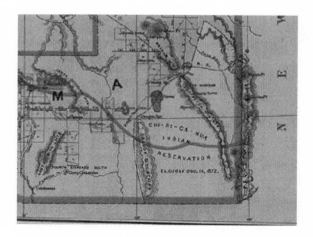

who was a political ally of Jesse James somehow had treasure that ended up in Victorio's Peak. Much of this was speculation but it was a potential connection to the KGC that Ben was interested in since he was related to Jesse James and also possibly Chief Victorio.

Ben began retracing the steps of the "Apache Wolf" aka Chief Victorio to see If there is any potential truth behind the rumors of a faked death. Most of those involved with doing research for the tribe were under the impression that the rumors were mainly coming from Gringo or white man accounts for whatever reason and were seriously lacking credibility. However, to Ben the fact that the rumors were coming from white men seemed to echo a possible KGC connection because an Indian faking his death is not something white men would normally brag about or even talk about in the first place unless they were somehow connected. How do you like them apples?

It was said that the so called James Gang, Quantrill's Guerillas led by the famous William Clarke Quantrill, and the Missouri Confederate Irregulars under General Marmaduke or General J. O. Shelby, where nothing more than a secret underground Confederate Army operating secretly throughout the South and Southwestern United States. This was the same Gen. Shelby that led his troops into Mexico to help the proclaimed French foreign leader, Emperor Maximilian. Unfortunately Gen. Shelby's expedition proved to be a disaster and it was necessary for the Knights of the Golden Circle to send in an experienced guerrilla force under Col. Jesse W. James and William Quantrill to rescue what was left

of Shelby's Army around 3,200 men. It was also said that the Hapsburg Jewels and heirlooms entrusted

to Maximilian by Napoleon Bonaparte including the Emperor's personal wealth and a great Aztec

treasure vault, were secured by the Confederate's and moved into a cavern in a very large and famous

peak in the San Andre's range of New Mexico.

Benito Juarez, the liberator of Mexico and his so-called patriots captured Emperor Maximilian and

executed him and his entire staff by firing squad.

After the close of the Civil War the Knight's of the Golden Circle moved very quickly to establish a

foothold in very profitable businesses throughout the country. They set up movies houses, livery

stables, a clever ploy, mining companies, timber companies and railroad contracting operations. They

even started a chain of drug stores, not to shabby as it's hard to fight a second civil war without a good

source of drugs. Later on they moved into the banking business; wall street brokering, money

laundering and manufacturing. They would deposit large sums of money in K.G.C. banks, insure the

deposits thru Wall Street Brokers and Bankers and turn around, rob the money back and of course

collecting the full amount from the surety insurance companies.

They even continued the practice that they were most famous for which was stealing illegal contraband

and of course more sophisticated forms of robbery, a trade that they had perfected into a science.

Every venture had a military responsibility and specific purpose. Ben kept thinking about when the

Title Chief of the United States Rick Wilson had said to Ben that he needs to get ready for a fight.

Does all this sound like a bunch of hicks running around trying to stir up trouble, or does this sound

like a group of well trained military men who are planning a grand battle adventure to again fight their enemies, who officially defeated them in the first American Civil War according to known history.

All the south had to do was figure a way to finance it themselves.

It's a little known secret that the Knights of The Golden Circle established major treasure and goods depositories in every state in the United States plus Canada, Mexico and other places in Central and South America.

A list of many of the treasures and depositories buried by the Knights of the Golden Circle was listed in the book 'A Jesse James was one of his Names', by Del Schrader and his co-author Lee Hauk a.k.a. Jesse Lee James III. All of the information for this book was provided by Lee Hauk including the specific names and list of treasures provided in code.

The KGC had a very prescribed and detailed method to burying large treasure depositories. They were also known for leaving a very sophisticated and overlapping methods of signs, clues, and many other types of locating devices. Every treasure has a name that may or may not give a clue to where the treasure is located.

Certainly noted was that these treasures were not to be easily found by weekend treasure hunters but were meant to be located and opened by the right person or group of people.

It should be also noted that the KGC buried smaller treasures in the vicinity of large depositories in an effort to conceal and divert attention away from the major treasures or depositor.

Across Sonora in old Mexico to west Texas and across southern New Mexico, few names were as dreaded during the late 1870s as that of Victorio, the Mimbres (Warm Springs) Apache war chief. Considered by some to have been the most effective of all Apache war leaders, Victorio consistently outmaneuvered and outfought the military forces sent to oppose him from both sides of the border, despite the fact that he usually had women and children in his band. Like many other great captains in history, he possessed a natural instinct for the kind of swift hawk-like thrust that made him feared and hated by all who sought to destroy him. One American Army officer thought of him as the "greatest Indian general who ever appeared on the continent."

In physique, Victorio was a typical Apache, though perhaps burlier than most. Indian inspector John Kimball described him as being " short and stout with a heavy, firm-set lower jaw, and an eye of a politician. He was dressed in a grimy calico shirt and coarse trousers, and was without paint, feathers, or ornament of any kind."

Victorio is thought to have been born in the Black Range area of southwestern New Mexico, probably about 1825.

Little is known of Victorio's childhood, but by the 1850s he was beginning to emerge as a warrior of promise, honing his skills on numerous raids into Mexico. In those days, Apache war parties swept across the border regularly, to raid and plunder or to seek vengeance for atrocities inflicted on them by Mexicans.

It was an unforgiving time, with brutality rampant on both sides. Gold was discovered in southwestern New Mexico in 1860. This brought an invasion of White gold hunters who hunted the Apaches game, set up whiskey stills and totally disrupting the Indian way of life. The Apaches began attacking gold prospectors and raiding the ranchers livestock.

In December 1860, a party of miners attacked some peaceful Apaches on the Mimbres River in retaliation for a mule thought to have been stolen by Apaches. Later, the Army confiscated Apache stock to pay for what had been stolen from the miners. The incident angered Victorio and set him on the warpath.

When the Civil War erupted and drew most of the regular Army troops east, Victorio, like the other Apache leaders, took advantage of the situation to raid across the territory. It is likely that he was with Mangas Coloradas and Cochise at the Battle of Apache Pass in 1862.

After Mangas' death in 1863, Victorio gradually rose to prominence as the premier war chief among the

Eastern Chiricahua. Assembling a select group of warriors from both his own Warm Springs band and the Mescaleros, Victorio spent the next two years raiding through the Rio Grande Valley and down into Mexico.

By 1865, Victorio had grown weary of fighting and expressed a willingness to abandon his raiding ways and settle down, provided his people were given a suitable place to live. It was a situation that was to be repeated time and again. By 1870 the government had responded by establishing a reservation at Ojo Caliente that satisfied the Apaches. There they remained for some time in a more or less peaceable and contented state.

In 1877, in an effort to gain better control over the Apaches, the government decided that all bands should be concentrated on the San Carlos Reservation in eastern Arizona. The decision reflected poor or little understanding of the Apache culture. For one thing, the San Carlos area was hot, barren and unhealthy.

Moreover, not all Apache bands were friendly with one another, and merging them led to problems. Victorio reluctantly agreed to move, but then, in company with Loco, another prominent war leader, bolted from the reservation in early September.

The Apaches moved east, through the mountainous country of eastern Arizona, into New Mexico, raiding as they found opportunity. San Carlos police and a contingent of Apache scouts pursued them, but the raiders managed to stay just out of reach. By the end of the month, however, most had wearied of the business and surrendered at Fort Wingate, in northwestern New Mexico, asking only that they be allowed to return to Ojo Caliente, a request Colonel Edward Hatch, commanding the District of New Mexico, acceded to, provided the Apaches behaved themselves.

Victorio, however, was not yet ready to acquiesce. With a small band of followers he swept down into Mexico to resume raiding and terrorizing south of the border.

In February 1878, Victorio recrossed the border and turned himself in to authorities at Ojo Caliente, where he was allowed to remain while the Army and the Interior Department wrestled with the decision of where to put the Apaches.

For a time, some consideration was given to sending them to Fort Sill, Indian Territory (present-day Oklahoma). In October, however, it was finally decided to send them back to San Carlos. Once again Victorio struck south, this time with about 80 warriors, while the rest of the Warm Springs band under Loco trudged back to the hated San Carlos.

The scenario was a repeat of the previous year. After a winter spent slipping back and forth between Chihuahua and New Mexico, Victorio returned in February 1879, requesting that he and his warriors be allowed to stay at Ojo Caliente but he was amenable to almost anyplace except San Carlos. After considering the matter, the government in its wisdom, again chose the Mescalero Reservation.

At first Victorio balked but he later consented, as long as his warriors' families could rejoin them from San Carlos and the government agreed.

In September 1879, word reached Victorio that authorities in Silver City New Mexico Territory had charged him with murder and horse stealing. Certain they would be coming after him, Victorio gathered his band together and once more headed into the mountains, where, in the months ahead, he would be joined by other discontented Mescalero and Chiricahua raiders. For Victorio, there would be no return.

With the news that Victorio was again on the loose the Army spread a network of patrols across southeastern Arizona and southwestern New Mexico. Victorio cunningly avoided those areas but the patrols skill found him. When columns of troops tried to penetrate his stronghold in the Mimbres Mountains west of present-day Truth and Consequences, N.M., he struck savagely.

In September 1879, Victorio and some 150 warriors ambushed a patrol of Colonel Hatch's 9th Cavalry, including a contingent of Navajo scouts. The fight was a tough, daylong affair, with the troops losing eight killed and two wounded, as well as a number of horses and mules, before they were able to extricate themselves.

The action foreshadowed what the fall held in store as Victorio demonstrated his innate skills as a guerrilla leader time and again. In November, a Mexican force of 50 frontiersmen was ambushed in the Candeleria Mountains and nearly wiped out. Their casualties amounted to 32 killed and 18 wounded. Up and down the southern Rio Grande valley and across the border Victorio and his band rode, appearing suddenly to raid and burn before disappearing into the tawny distance from which they had emerged. On both sides of the border, military units seemed helpless.

In Arizona, General Orlando Willcox had his units covering the southeastern sector of that territory, while Hatch ordered all units of the 9th Cavalry to southern New Mexico but Victorio continued to prove elusive. On those rare occasions when they managed to find him, they usually had ample cause to regret having done so.

Early in 1880, Victorio again came north across the border. Troop detachments from both Arizona and New Mexico pursued with a vigor that did produce several engagements with the Apaches but resulted in little more than a few casualties and considerable frustration.

In late March 1880, Hatch launched a carefully laid campaign for which he entertained high hopes.

With reports indicating that Victorio was holed-up in Hembrillo Canyon, in the San Andreas Mountains, Hatch moved east from Aleman with a strong column, while a second force moved down from Fort Stanton. Yet a third column under Brig. Gen. Benjamin Grierson would move in from west Texas to seal off escape in that direction.

The Fort Stanton column, commanded by Captain Henry Carroll, had the unenviable chore of moving across the dreaded malpais ("badlands") country. Carroll and his men found themselves barely able to function after drinking water heavily laden with gypsum. When the wretchedly ill troops surprised Victorio's camp, the Apaches quickly perceived that all was not well with the soldiers and promptly turned the tables, pinning down Carroll's force.

Fortunately, part of Hatch's command arrived to relieve the suffering and beleaguered soldiers. The rescue, however, allowed Victorio to escape, though narrowly missed Hatch's main column in doing so.

The constant strain of pursuit was beginning to wear down even the indefatigable Apaches. The Mescalero reservation had been a source of supplies for Victorio with weapons, ammunition. horses and other necessities. Recognizing that, the Army sealed off the corridor, reducing the Apaches to replacing their inventories from what could be reaped from their raids on ranches.

In May 1880, a detachment of Apache scouts under a hard-bitten chief of scouts, H.K. Parker, succeeded in surprising Victorio's camp in Palomas Canyon north of present-day Hillsboro, N.M. Parker's command was not strong enough to overpower the Apaches; he rushed a courier off to Hatch, requesting support, but was finally compelled to withdraw when none was forthcoming. Why Hatch did not respond with alacrity is unclear, but he suffered severe criticism at the hands of the local press. Nevertheless, the fight had been costly for the Apaches, who lost a number of warriors. Victorio himself was reportedly wounded in the leg. As always, though, once the smoke of battle had dissipated, the Apaches had vanished.

The Army continued its dogged pursuit. Detachments of troops were placed at all known water holes, but Victorio's skill at avoiding these traps remained uncannily sharp. Sometimes, though, even a cagey warrior such as Victorio discovered that things were not always what they seemed. In August 1880, he attacked what appeared to be a fat and promising unprotected Army supply train at Rattlesnake Springs, Texas, only to be suddenly confronted by the train's escort, which had been riding inside. The soldiers promptly piled out to confront and drive off the Apaches.

In October 1880, U.S. and Mexican troops located Victorio's hideaway in the Tres Castillo's Mountains of Mexico. Ordering the U.S. forces to leave, the Mexicans attacked the Apache stronghold, killing all but 17 of the band. Victorio was one of the dead men. The Apaches believed Victorio took his own life, while others said that a Tarahumara Indian scout working for the Mexicans killed the Apache leader. Although the survivors of Tres Castillo's insisted that Victorio had died in the fighting, rumors of his escape persisted. This is where Ben plugged the KGC into the equation who ultimately had control of the Mexican Army through Emperor Maximilian. The US Army never saw Victorio's body and rumor's persisted for potentially good reason.

But whether he perished at Tres Castillo's or not, it may safely be said that Victorio left his imprint on the face of the Southwest. As biographer Thrapp suggested, he may well have been "America's greatest guerrilla fighter." Ben concluded based on his investigation of the KGC in the southwest and his own family information of the Chiricahua moving to southern Mexico and the new information on Jesse W James all seem to indicate that Victorio faked his death. Victorio was noted by the US military

themselves as being very politically inclined with a firm eye, a bit more shorter but a more burly frame than most, a very prominent jawbone, and a simple appearance of trousers and a shirt but no war paint or decorations of any kind. What Ben read about Victorio all seemed to paint the picture of a very politically active individual and leader which is exactly what Colonel Jesse W James specialized in as well.

Ben reviewed several accounts of treasure located near Victorio's Peak.

In the book Ancient Civilizations the author recited his views on Victorio's peak after saying that there were a few KGC symbols found in the area and maybe some treasure but that was small potatoes compared to the labyrinth of tunnels underneath the mountain.

"My own belief is that Victorio Peak began as an ancient civilization, perhaps of Aztec or Olmec Indians, or perhaps a civilization of whom there is no knowledge in recorded history. These original people mined a vein of gold and lived in the network of tunnels and caverns beneath the Peak.'"

"'They flourished with the wild game and running water which was abundant in the Hembrillo Basin. This was likely more than 1,000 years ago. The ancient language of Ogam, more than a thousand years old, has been found scrawled on rocks within the confines of the Hembrillo Basin.'"

"'After the extinction of these original inhabitants, whoever they were, the site was lost to the world for perhaps many centuries. But legends of such an imaginary place, an El Dorado, or City of Gold, were handed down by word of mouth, and the search for it never ceased.'"

During the search for the KGC connection to the Apaches Ben was asked by several family

members on his native American side of the family to help with acquiring CDIB cards which stands for

Certified Degree of Indian Blood.

The first issue Ben realized was that his family belonged to 2 different tribes and neither one was

federally recognized. The Piro from West Texas have been in Socorro, Texas since 1680 and only some

Chiricahua Apache had been federally recognized as prisoners of war after Geronimo had laid down his

rifle. To complicate matters some of Ben's relatives were born in Mexico but were descendants of the

Piro tribe from west Texas. To complicate things even worse was the fact that there was a civil war

going on in Mexico and these relatives asked Ben to help get them access to their tribal land in Texas.

Ben ran the story by Rick Wilson the Chief of Title Matters who had already helped on the giant J situation. Rick said the native American issue is very sensitive and appreciates that Ben wants to help them out but that is strictly an issue for the Bureau of Indian Affairs or the office of Federal Acknowledgment.

The next thing Ben knew he was compiling the family land records to re-establish the 2 tribes and get his cousins their CDIB cards. His father had also inquired about a CDIB card for medical benefits so Ben prepared to submit the family historical information to the Office of Federal Acknowledgment.

His family history and records showed that his 4th great grandfather Calisto Olguin was the owner of most of West Texas and may have been related to or at least associated with the Piro tribe.
Ben also acquired a map that was granted to the tribe by the King of Spain in 1680 before Mexico was Mexico and before Texas was Texas.

Calisto Olguin is listed as the primary last owner of over 65,000 acres on the 1860 census. This map also contained the Guadalupe Mountains which was a known Apache stronghold for Chief Victorio in the 1860's when Calisto Olguin was possibly considered the Piro Chief.

Ben also found the map for the Chiricahua Apache that was rescinded in 1872 just six months after being signed into effect by Presidential executive order.

The Chiricahua Apache Reservation was the largest in North America and consisted of SE Arizona which was Cochise's Band, SW New Mexico which was Victorio's Band, and pretty much all of

Northern Mexico .

The golden circle the KGC were referring to was suppose to extend from the Southeast to the Southwest to Mexico and also the Caribbean.

Their apparent stated agenda to create another slave empire in the Southwest could have very well been a cover story for their real agenda. Ben didn't buy into the fact that a very secret military order would announce their agenda so openly and which obviously got recoded in history as such.

It made much more sense that the real golden circle they were talking about was the Black Hills and is today considered the wealthiest 100 square miles on earth.

Ben was very interested in the possible Victorio connection because his 2nd great grandfather Victorio was a Chiricahua Apache and was born in 1880 the same year Victorio supposedly died.

It also excepted among the tribe that because Victorio left the reservation it is not possible to know for sure how many children he had as the Apaches did not keep written records. Ben sent his family information to a current Chiricahua Chief named Manny Sonchos who was representing over 1000 people that considered themselves Chiricahua from southern and northern California and all over the entire Southwest.

Manny was also a Federal Agent on Indian Reservations in the southwest U.S. ironically and had been working with other members of the tribe on Genealogy for many people.

He told Ben that his researchers had determined based on the info Ben provided that Ben was either directly related to the "Apache Wolf" Chief Victorio or to Victor Montoya who was part of the same Band so either way Ben was considered a tribal member whether the tribe was federally recognized or not.

Ben was quite shocked to find out that the once largest reservation in north America is not even a recognized tribe anymore other than the 400 prisoners of war.

The potential Victorio cover up seemed to be an elusive trick the Apache Wolf pulled off in order to end a war against an entire group of people. If the Chief and his warriors were wiped out then the war would be almost over in 1880 if they could just find Geronimo and his remaining renegades.

Geronimo continued war until 1886 was most likely a diversion tactic originally which lasted much longer than probably originally anticipated. Geronimo and his warriors stayed in the field of battle for another 6 years while Victorio moved the people to safety into a mountainous region of southern Mexico near Jalisco. The Sierra Madres run from northern Mexico all the way to the pacific ocean in Jalisco and with the many indigenous populations of Mexico it would have been quite easy for the people to settle in for an extended period.

That is exactly where Ben's 2nd great Grandpa Victor Beltran was born and then Ben also found

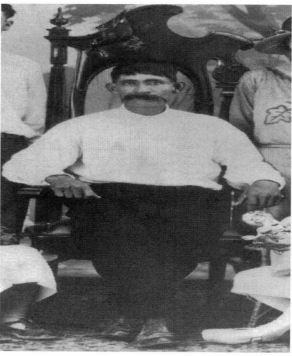

other evidence in an online genealogy forum where someone also had family from Jalisco that was

Chiricahua Apache.

Why would the Mexican Army want to assist an Apache renegade whose tribe had

killed countless Spanish trespassers?

The reason Ben thought was very simple indeed. Emperor Maximilian who controlled the Army

was certainly a known KGC political partner and personal friend of Jesse W James.

By 1880 Colonel Jesse W James was notorious for working with the American Indian leaders directly like the Sioux leader Sitting Bull and Cherokee Confederate General Stand Watie and many

many more.

There were also rumors that some of Maximilian treasure had ended up in Victorio's Peak

after a revolt which is really just another way of saying that Victorio was working with Maximilian

and Jesse James who apparently was paid quite handsomely in millions of dollars to assist in

Maximilian escape during a political revolt near Mexico City.

Ben was convinced that the Apache were working with the KGC by the year 1880 even though

they originally had fought against both the Confederate and Union Army at the onslaught of the Civil

War.

Ben was still waiting for the Special Agent from the Forest Service to get get back to him about the

giant J goldmine and for Citibank to respond about the gold reserves as well.

He continued work on compiling all the necessary historical background and family land records for

the Office of Federal Acknowledgment which would ultimately be in charge of granting federal

recognition to the Piro and Chiricahua tribes who have lived on their respective land for thousands of

years.

Ben got an email from Special Agent Tucker in Rapid City asking for Title Chief Rick Wilson's phone number and mentioning that he has not been able to get a hold him.

Ben called Rick Wilson the Chief of Title Matters for the United States and Rick picked up

the phone right away and said that he would be prepared for the Special Agents call. Ben started

thinking that the Agent was trying to buy time for some reason.

Maybe because the situation concerning the mineral patents is seriously a giant mess of corruption

they may need more time to sort through it all.

Ben went back to preparing a letter of petition and necessary documents for the Indian tribes federal

requirements to be recognized and receive benefits as well as citizenship possibly for the Indians that

live along the border that is now engaged in a brutal civil war in real time. By 2012 over 50,000

people had been killed in Mexico do to a Narco-Civil War between factions that are heavily reliant on

trade routes that run through ancestral Chiricahua Apache territory.

The political environment in Mexico is much different than the USA do to a population that is 90%

indigenous to some degree. 60% of the people are a mix of American Indian and Caucasian, 30% of the

people are 100% American Indian, and the remainimg10% of the people are Caucasian, African, and

whatever else.

The cultures and history of Mexico is much different than the USA and the ancestral roots of the

American Indian tribes are honored and cherished by the majority of Mexican people but they are also still shunned by the political Spanish element and by the Indians own illiterate poverty level populations that buy into the Spanish brainwash campaign which originally started with the forced acceptance and perception of Christianity. Although many Indians converted to Christianity the forced idea of anything did not sit well with many of the tribal peoples and therefore had always been part of a Spanish political agenda to some extent in the Southwest and Mexico.

It was ultimately the US Army coming into Mexico that ended the Apache wars. The Spanish nor the Apache wanted the US on Mexican soil so they faked the death of Victorio and sent the Army away.

Chief Victorio was a huge political power and was the last Chief in North America to roam freely with up to 500 warriors at a single time. Ben compared pictures of his 2nd great grandpa Victor to Chief Victorio and the resemblance is undeniable. Victorio's jawline is a huge square and distinctively different than Geronimo's jawline. The jaw of Chief Victorio who would be Ben's 3rd great grandfather is identical to his 2nd great grandfather Victor Beltran born in Jalisco, Mexico 1880.

It makes sense that Jesse W James would want to make an alliance with the Apaches because they were and still are without a doubt the most bad ass guerilla fighters that ever lived. When Jesse James sold guns to the Apaches he probably didn't need to give out much training whatsoever. The Apaches were notorious just like Jesse James for acquiring the best fire power by any means necessary even if they had to ride all the way to Kansas they were going to be coming home with the best repeating rifles available because Apache territory was always a constant battleground.

It had become clear to Ben that the KGC and the Confederate Army went underground in 1865 and still haven't emerged from the shadows until right now!

Ben get's a call from Carl Hobie his treasure hunting buddy and Carl seemed optimistic about Citibank but said there was no way this story would ever turn into a book unless he get's the giant J back or get's a billion dollars from the Fed.

If the KGC won the Civil war through the banking system and built the Federal Reserve then where are they now Ben's friend Carl Hobie asked?

Ben said they are all dead Carl because the Civil War was over a century ago but their descendants are alive and running the show now. The Fed is really just another name for the Confederate treasury but even the Fed was not the entire treasure.

Ben waited to hear back from Special Agent Tucker or Citibank. He was there. He was finally there at the end of the "Black Eagle".

This long journey and quest of the giant J has led to this final moment of mystery and suspense.

Ben is still waiting......He prepares the Federal petition for his Indian tribes as he waits....He gathers his essential survival gear in case he needs to go live in a cave like the real Jesse James.

What if Citibank was going to hijack his gold just like the county had stolen his giant J goldmine? He

may have no choice but to live in hiding for the rest of his life just like Jesse W. James.

The financial situation in the economy is not good with many experts saying a Global

depression could take place in 2012.

The government moves slower than an 8 day clock. Ben continues to wait patiently......All he wants is

access to his family property.

Get the hell off my Giant J he yelled into the wind!!!!! To Ben the land was spiritual and is where part

of his bloodline was created.

Those mountains and those streams were every bit apart of his spirit.

The Giant J was his family's home and a place that they carved out of the wilderness over 100 years

ago.

The Comptroller
Chapter 11

Ben Miller is still waiting for access to his family's Giant J goldmine property and to hear from

Citibank about the massive investment into the Federal Reserve . In doing further research Ben found

out that Citibank was bailed out during the 2008 financial crisis and was completely controlled by the

Comptroller of the Currency.

Very ironic? Coincidental? Probably not! Ben Miller aka Jesse W James VII meets the active

Comptroller and asks for his gold back. Ironically, Comptroller of the Currency is exactly what Jesse

W James did for the KGC and the Confederate Army.

Ben is looking for the gold deposit that was made by Colonel Jackson via Citibank into the New

York Fed which is the documented first contributor to the Federal Reserve System.

Ben called the Comptroller's office or OCC and was told to fill out some forms and that an

investigation would be handled by the Consumer Financial Protection Bureau. Ben was shocked! He

said you mean I have to start another investigation to get my gold back? Ultimately the power of

Andrew Jackson's power was not an illusion when he "Killed the Bank".

Andrew's cousins who were also named Colonel Jackson were burdened with building a new system

which led to the creation of the Federal Reserve. There was nobody on the planet with more gold than

Colonel Jackson C. Jackson when the Fed was created because he had the Confederate treasure and the

Giant J gold mine aka Cibola located in the middle of the wealthiest 100 square miles on planet earth.

Ben knew there was a fight going on but he also knew that it was going to be damn near impossible to

steal Colonel Jackson's investment in the Fed. Gold doesn't just fall out of the sky and treasures don't

disappear either. Ben was amazed how far this Quest of the Giant J has come and is still

evolving.

Ben finished preparing his supporting documents for the federal tribal recognition process and

submitted them on behalf of 2 separate Native American tribes located in the Southwestern United

States. Although his initial petition was denied for not meeting the federal criteria Ben is continuing his efforts to work with his families tribes for their further development of cultural and heritage

preservation and recognition. He was still completely amazed that the largest Indian tribe in north

America has still not been recognized to this day. How could they have the largest reservation in North

America one day and then not exist at all he next day?

While working on the Quest of the Giant J Ben got a call from Bill

Bentley that mysterious record producer who was formerly the

Senior Vice President of Warner Bros Music when he first called in 2005 after Ben's second album

release.

The music man was now the A&R Director at Vanguard Records and had just signed Merle Haggard

who has had 40 #1 top hits over his lengthy music career. The legendary producer asked Ben if he

would Co-write a song with him called " The Fire Next Time" which is partly themed around the

biblical prophecy of the end times as well as the economic chaos and massive bailout's of cash that

the Bush administration had squandered. The song was was released on i-tunes and CDBaby in 2011.

Ben also released 4 new songs in early 2012 and he is still busy writing and recording album #5.

Ben wasn't much for politics but he knew enough about Andrew Jackson and the family now

to realize that there would certainly be a fight if someone tries to steal Colonel Jackson's gold.

It was truly Ben's perseverance and the tenacious tracking ability instilled in his blood through "Genetic Memory" transformation by his Apache ancestors, Jesse James, and Colonel Jackson that guided him in this spectacular "Quest of the Giant J".

The "Quest of the Giant J" is what led Ben to discover his blood relation to President/General Andrew Jackson and Lt. General Stonewall Jackson and also discovering the truth about the the 2 Generals relation to each other that historians have debated for 150 years.

The Giant J is ultimately what led to the discovery of the true unknown identity of Colonel Jesse Woodson James who is Ben's 4th great grandfather and has also been a controversial mystery for 150 years.

The Giant J is what led Ben to discover the location of the Confederate treasure and the construction of the Federal Reserve system.

The Giant J is what led to the discovery of massive nationwide theft and fraud involving private mineral wealth that was issued to the original settlers and pioneers in the form of Federal Mineral patents that retain federal jurisdiction through conditions and stipulations of sale and are not subject to property tax or state control. The massive theft of these properties has led to mortgage fraud, title fraud, damage and destruction to private property, insurance fraud and government corruption. The theft of the Giant J is what forced the US government to address the situation as to how the counties have been allowed to steal these private properties located in Federal jurisdiction which is potentially thousands of properties issued in the form of federal mineral patents all over the west. Ben found several other mineral patents issued to other family members that had also appeared to be stolen by the counties in which they are all trespassing on private property in federal jurisdiction.

As Ben's cousin General Andrew Jackson would surely say, we might just have to send in the Tennessee Militia because he who holds the gold makes the rules and that is our gold.

Bob Brewer the renowned expert on the KGC had said that if Ben was right about the federal laws in the mineral patents it would change history.

Ben assured Bob that the laws were federal and that they kept the property under "exclusive federal legislative jurisdiction".

Ben explained to his friend Carl that he was in the process of re-writing history.

Ben had clearly come to the realization that there were 2 Jesse James and 2 Frank James that were cousins just like J. Frank Dalton said. There were known photos of the 2 pairs of brothers as well which were obviously not the same people in both photos. Ben had been doing research in Oklahoma and stumbled across the land patents that were issued to Jesse and Frank James when they married into the Sac Fox Indian tribe.

Years after Jesse Woodson James faked his death in 1882 Missouri his cousins Jesse Robert James and Frank James were still laying low and were really the ones from Missouri but the name Jesse Robert James never surfaced and the body was identified by several officials in Clay County that knew Jesse James so it was never questioned. By the 1880's the photo's of Jesse Robert James were authenticated as being Jesse Woodson James when in reality they were completely different people. The confusion was added by the fact that they were both members of the KGC and the secret Confederate underground Army. The James boys did not care to set the record straight that there were actually multiple Jesse James' and multiple Frank James'.

Ben used his Apache tracking skills to track Jesse Woodson James to the Black Hills and then to California where they visited their cousin Drury Woodson James who had invested in a large luxury hotel.

Ben was searching through land patents in Oklahoma and just so happen to stumble across the patents issued to Jesse and Frank James when the married into the Sac Fox tribe.

The patent had an Indian name listed with the James brothers patents. Ben could not believe his eyes.

The name on the patent with Frank James was Ketch-e-maw. Ben had been looking into the family

name Ketchpaw or something close for over 10 years with no luck at all. He thought it was Native

American sounding but could not find anything and now he is starring at Ketch-e-Mah. He called the

tribe and found out that Jesse James his cousin had 2 children and named his son Frank. They said that

Ben currently has cousins that are blood members of the Sac Fox tribe. The office did not have

information on Frank James but confirmed without a doubt that Ketch-e-Mah was the Indian name for

Frank James. Ben's gun and Retired Sgt of Chicago Police badge has been hanging in his office for

over 10 years.

It had writing on the back of the frame from another cousin decades before that said Officer

Marshall Ketchpaw or Kitchpao was the owner but was not really sure of the spelling obviously.

Ben had just seen a picture of Billy the Kid sell for 2.3 million dollars in a wild west auction.

Frank James was known to be a lawman in the wild west and went under the name of Frank Jackson at

some point in Kansas supposedly. Jesse and Frank also supposedly married into an Indian Tribe.

Ben has been able to verify more supposed situations than not and most of the time the myths or

legends are true concerning Jesse and Frank James but which Jesse and Frank is the real tricky part most of the time.

Some of the stories are impossible to tell which Jesse James or Frank James they are talking about but most of the time Ben was able to figure it out based on the vast age differences between the cousins.

Ben knew that Ketch-e-mah was extremely unique and if he could verify that the badge belonged to Ketch-e-mah then he could prove that Ketch-e-mah was actually Frank James based on the land patent and tribal records. Ben called the Chicago Police and was lucky to find someone who was willing to search the records for him but it could take a week or so. The badge and gun that were previously valued at a $400 are now potentially worth millions of dollars in the wild west collectors market. What would you rather have a picture of Billy the Kid where only 4 are known to exist or would you rather have the an actual badge and gun that belonged to the notorious Outlaw Frank James when he became a Chicago Police Sgt and was the older brother to Jesse James of Missouri and cousins to the legendary Colonel Jesse Woodson James. The picture of the fort with Colonel Jackson and Jesse W. James could also be worth millions in the wild west collectors market especially if Jesse W. James is positively identified in the photo of course as an old man.

Ben contacted the Chicago history museum who was able to verify that there was an officer Ketchpaw who served at least until 1904. Ben found records on the census showing him serving on the police force starting in 1889 and prior to that he was listed as a milk dealer. Ben had also verified that

other historians had identified Jesse and Frank from Missouri on the 1880 Nashville, Tn census with

Frank going by the name Ben J. Woodson and Jesse was listed as Geo Howard. Frank's wife was listed

as Fannie Woodson and Jesse's wife was listed as Josie Howard.

1880 United States Federal Census

Ben. J. Woodson
40
abt 1840
Maryland
District 23, Davidson, Tennessee
White
Male
Self (Head)

Married
Fannie Woodson
Maryland

Maryland

Farmer

Name	Age
Ben. J. Woodson	40
Fannie Woodson	27
Robert Woodson	2
Geo. D. Howard	32
Josie Howard	29
Charles Howard	4
Mary Howard	1

Frank and his wife was listed as having one child named Robert Woodson.

Jesse and wife Josie were listed with a boy and girl which also matches up to the tribes account of him having 2 children.

Ben could clearly see that these ages were certainly a match to his cousins Jesse and Frank from

Missouri.

In the 1880's the real Jesse Woodson James and his brother Frank had been documented as

being in the far northwest and in California at a hotel called Paso Robles owned by their 1st cousin

Drury Woodson James who was a wealthy uncle of the Missouri James boys and brother to their father

Robert Sallee James. The hotel still has a floor dedicated to Jesse Woodson James.

At this point in history both cousins were famous regardless of who was really who and they were all

comrades in arms in the post civil war reconstruction period .

By the mid 1870's Ben had tracked his cousin's Frank and the Missouri born Jesse Robert James aka

		Land Patent Details	
Accession Nr : OK1060___.A_0	Document Type: State Volume Patent	State: Oklaho

Names On Document		Miscellan-	
☑ NUM-ME-AW-SHE-KO,	Land Office:	Washington Ofc
☑ JAMES JESSE	US Reservations:	No
	Mineral Reservations:	No
	Tribe:	---
	Militia:	
	State In Favor Of:	---
Military Rank: ---	Authority:	February 8, 1887; Indian Allotm

Document Numbers		Surve
Document Nr: 0	Total Acres: 160.00
Misc. Doc. Nr: ---	Survey Date:
BLM Serial Nr: ---	Geographic Name: ---
Indian Allot. Nr: ---	Metes/Bounds: No

Num-Me-Aw-She-Ko to the Sac Fox tribe in Oklahoma while Jesse Woodson James was in the far west

making alliances with Sitting Bull and the other western plains tribes.

After the faked death in 1882 of Colonel Jesse Woodson James the Missouri James boys split up with

Jesse Robert James staying in Oklahoma with his wife and 2 children on the Indian Reservation.

Alexander Franklin James from Missouri was given the Indian name Ketch-

e-mah and appears to have taken up the identity of a Marshall Ketchpaw in the late 1870's as a milk

dealer and then became a police Sgt in Chicago watching over the treasure in the massive tunnel

system built by his cousin Colonel Jackson C. Jackson.

Ben received notice from the Chicago Historical Society that they have personnel files for an

officer Marshall Ketchpaw from 1897-1904.

1904 was also around the same time that Colonel Jackson began closing down the goldmine operation

and moved his family back to Chicago where many of the tunnels had already been constructed covertly under the direction of his brother and Chief tunnel engineer George

Washington Jackson.

Frank James became an Indian named Ketch-e-mah and then became Marshall

Ketchpaw from 1880 forward using several spelling variations including Ketchsaw, Ketchpow,

Kitchpan, Ketchpone, Ketchbow, Ketchemah,etc. He also used several first names as well including

Wert, Martin, Marchel,

	Lan(
Accession Nr: OK1060___.452	**Document Type:** State Volur
Names On Document	
KETCH-E-MAH, JAMES, FRANK	**Land Office:** Was
	US Reservations: No
	Mineral Reservations: No
	Tribe:
	Militia:
	State In Favor Of:
Military Rank:	**Authority:** Febr
Document Numbers	
Document Nr: 0	**Total Acres:** 160.

Marshall, Marshal and of course Frank.

Marshall Ketchpaw or Ketchemah had a son named Frank Ketchpaw and a daughter named

Mabel. Frank Ketchpaw Jr had a daughter named Jesse Ketchpaw.

Ben was stunned as he studied the ages of these people and it was clear to Ben that Frank James

from Missouri never married Annie Ralston and that his real wife was really from Chicago. Franks

fake wife Annie Raltson was a KGC operative that apparently pretended to be married to Frank James who was then sitting in jail waiting for his pardon but really he was also not the real Frank James and

was also a paid KGC operative that was playing along waiting for Annie to negotiate his pardon with

the Governor.

The real Frank James from Missouri was living in Chicago but also had land in Oklahoma near

his brother Jesse Robert James who was living under his Indian name given to him by the Sac Fox

tribe.

Frank James faked his death in 1915 and continued retirement in Chicago occasionally flashing his

Retired Sgt of Police badge when needed.

Ben's grandma had acquired the badge and gun from her 2nd cousin

who was the granddaughter of Frank James aka Ketchemah

aka Marshall Ketchpaw.

Ben thought about the fact that he had the badge and gun from Frank James all this time sitting in

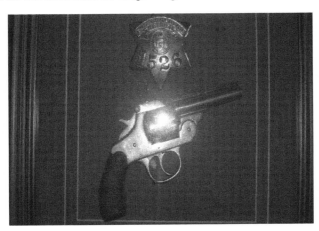

his office and a picture of the Giant J goldmine that most likely included Jesse Woodson James

many years after his supposed assassination by Bob Ford.

Unbelievable! Inconceivable! Essentially both Jesses and Franks lived under new identities for the rest

of their lives in peace.

Frank was now pardoned and Jesse was legally dead so there was nothing else more for the authorities

to do but close the investigations.

It was the Quest of the Giant J that ultimately led Ben to finally discover the true identity of his cousin

Frank James aka Ketch-e-maw aka Marshall Ketchpaw.

Many theories have come forth about the possibility that Jesse Woodson James faked his death which Ben has proven just based on clearing up the simple fact that Jesse R James from Missouri on the 1850 census was clearly not Jesse Woodson James and the fact that Frank James from Missouri also faked his death at age 72 is now a completely new addition to the legend of Jesse James and the secret military order of the KGC.

"Jesse James Was One His Names" by Del Schrader asserted that Jesse W. James had 72 identities over his life span. Frank's alias Marshall Ketchpaw lived to be 80 but in reality Frank James was 89 years old in 1932 when he passed away in Chicago. There was even an autobiography written by a man named Joe Vaughn who claimed to be the Outlaw Frank James. Joe stated in his book that the man who sat in jail for a year was paid to impersonate Frank James until a pardon could be negotiated. Joe Vaughn's story that was eerily similar to J. Frank Dalton in a different light but again possibly designed to divulge KGC secrets to only the descendants who would understand the information. Joe Vaughn also claimed that Frank James never married Annie Ralston and Annie was really a KGC operative who was also paid to play along with the marriage to a man who was not really Frank James at all.

It certainly appeared that Joe Vaughn's autobiography matched up with what Ben had discovered. Ben

concluded that Joe Vaughn aka Frank James who died in 1926 was certainly not the real Frank James

but just like J. Frank Dalton had claimed to be Jesse James they both had some

corresponding information that was truly authentic in theory. The real Frank James who was Ben's

uncle from Tennessee most likely assumed a new identity like his cousin's from Missouri but Ben was

unable to locate him for sure although he did come up with a potential match of identity to him as well

but without any corresponding evidence it will have to remain a mystery.

The fact that both Franks and both Jesse's essentially faked their deaths and assumed new

identities and then built the Federal Reserve is completely rewriting history in a new light altogether. It

is "simply incredible" Ben exclaimed as he began compiling a scrap book of information that was

getting thicker and thicker as he continued his "Quest of the Giant J". Ben again began thinking about

getting access to his giant J goldmine property and he was still waiting to hear back from Special

Agent Tucker and the Comptroller of the Currency about the trillions of dollars worth of treasure and

gold in the Federal Reserve but at this point he was pretty confident that the comptroller will find

Colonel Jackson's massive gold deposits. The lingering question concerning the gold was that of a

potential collapse of the US Dollar which appeared to be lingering in mainstream consciousness

during the "Quest of the Giant J". It was obvious that the original intention of the Federal Reserve was

to keep the banking sector privately controlled by a central banking system but the extreme amounts of

debt that the US government had racked up in a relative short time in just the last 20 years has pushed

the country past the point of no return. The corrupt corporate interests that had taken over the

government had essentially bankrupt the country for generations to come. Ben was perplexed and was

recognizing just what dire straits the country was facing in reality. He felt an overwhelming amount of

responsibility to his ancestors and to the country but was unsure of a solution. Due to hyperinflation the

value of the US Dollar was spinning out of control and there was no end in sight of the spending with

Americans borrowing .40 cents for every dollar they spend. Meanwhile the government was trying to

keep Ben off his Giant J goldmine property while the price of gold was going through the roof.

It was starting to look like sending the Tennessee Militia Special Forces to secure the Giant J in the

midst of an economic collapse may be the only answer and one that his ancestors would certainly approve of if no other options exist. After several calls to cousins in Tennessee the Stonewall Jackson

Brigade was activated across many states during the summer of 2011. Time was running out. The

people had been defrauded and were preparing to fight tyranny on US soil once again.

Ben just so happened to type Jesse James and the Federal Reserve into the internet and up popped an

article called "How Jesse James, the Telegraph, and the Federal Reserve Act of 1913 can help the Army

win the war on terrorism". This article was a current military review of the economic environment in

Afghanistan and Iraq and how it corresponds to the insurgent guerilla attacks performed by Jesse James

which ultimately led to a safer central banking system called the Federal Reserve. Ben thought this was

very interesting. A current military article connecting Jesse James and the Federal Reserve?

http://usacac.army.mil/CAC2/MilitaryReview/Archives/English/MilitaryReview_20081231_art013.pdf

Very strange indeed but it did not mention the KGC or their direct involvement in actually creating the

Fed but it did basically say that the activities of Jesse James is what led to the Federal Reserve's

creation.

Ben compared the photos of Jesse Woodson James (above)and Benjamin Franklin James from West Tennessee with the known photos of Jesse Robert James (below) and Alexander Franklin James aka Ketch-e-maw from Missouri. Although historians have continually mistaken the 2 sets of cousins as being the same people it was quite obvious to Ben that they were not the same people. Ben also concluded that the photos above of the Tennessee James boys were taken in the 1840's that match the style and time period of the last known photo of General Andrew Jackson from Nashville in 1845 . Jesse W James above born in 1819 and was in his mid twenties in the 1840"s and Jesse R James below was born in 1847 and Alexander Franklin James in 1843.

Ben noted both photos taken in the Nashville area probably in the 1850's.. Benjamin Franklin James and Jesse Woodson James in their mid -thirties. The KGC headquarters remained in Nashville until the early 1880's when it was moved west. Historians have incorrectly labeled these photos as the Missouri James boys with Frank age 22 and Jesse age 19 and suggesting they were taken in 1865. The fact of the matter, is that Colonel Jesse Woodson James of the KGC was active during the civil war and the KGC was certainly not commanded by a teenager. As established by Ben, the 1850 census below suggests that these photos were taken prior to the civil war while Benjamin Franklin James and Jesse Woodson James were in their thirties. Furthermore , The **daguerreotype** /dəˈgerətaɪp/ (French: *daguerréotype*) process (also called **daguerreotypy**), introduced in 1839, was the first publicly announced photographic process and the first to come into widespread use. By the early 1860s, later processes which were less costly and produced more easily viewed images with shorter exposure times had almost entirely replaced it. These photos are consistent with the 1850' time frame and the Daguerreotype process.

Name:	**J W James**	
Age:	30	
Estimated Birth Year:	abt 1820	
Birth Place:	Tennessee	
Gender:	Male	
Home in 1850 (City,County,State):	District 18, Gibson, Tennessee	
Family Number:	1870	
Household Members:	Name	Age
	J W James	30
	Lucinda James	33
	Rebecca James	11
	George James	10
	William James	6
	Allen James	3
	G B Mcwhorter	67

Kentucky Historical Society

FRANK JAMES

The above photos are part of the Pence Historical Collection in Kentucky. It is clear that Frank and Jesse Woodson James have the same chair in the photo in Kentucky and Ben can clearly tell that this Jesse Woodson James looks nothing like his cousin Jesse Robert James from Missouri. Also noted is that both Frank and Jesse in these Kentucky pictures are certainly taller than 6ft while Jesse from Missouri was 5ft 8inches tall and Frank was slightly taller. These photos also support the time frame of the James boys from Tennessee being in their early 20's in the 1840's.

The **daguerreotype** /dəˈɡɛrətaɪp/ (French: *daguerréotype*) process (also called **daguerreotypy**), introduced in 1839, was the first publicly announced photographic process and the first to come into widespread use. By the early 1860s, later processes which were less costly and produced more easily viewed images with shorter exposure times had almost entirely replaced it.

This allegedly authenticated known Nashville photo shows Jesse Woodson James is over 6 ft tall and is wearing the same jacket and vest /shirt as in the chair picture from Kentucky. Frank is wearing an officers uniform showing 3 stars on the collar. Again, Jesse Robert James from Missouri was 5 ft 8

This rare portrait was taken in Nashville, Tennessee, at the close of the Civil War. It shows (left to right) Charles F. (Fletch) Taylor of Platte County, Wisconsin, a member of the Quantrill Guerrillas; Frank James in Confederate uniform showing three stars on the collar; and Jesse James, not yet 20.

inches tall and Frank James from Missouri would have been 21 or 22 years old in 1864-1865. The fact of the matter, is that nobody really had an age profile for the James boys of west Tennessee and Benjamin Franklin (Frank) James was actually born in 1817 and much older than Alexander Franklin James/Ketchemah born in 1843. Benjamin Franklin James grew up in west Tennessee and was a Confederate Officer in command of troops during the civil war and his home was located at the Grand

Ole Opry Theater on Fatherland Dr in Nashville which was also the headquarters for the Confederate Secret Service. If this photo was taken in 1865 then Frank James was 48 years old and Jesse Woodson James was 46 being born in 1819. The Kentucky connection is interesting and is the source of the true relation between the Missouri and Tennessee cousins. Ben's family tree shows that his 5th great grandfather Jesse Woodson James father was Robert L. James of Gibson, Tennessee born 1787 in Brunswick, Virginia. Ben's 6th great grandfather and Robert James father was John Peace James Sr. born 1755 in Brunswick, Virginia. John Peace James Sr. was a brother to John M. James who is the father of Robert Sallee James and grandfather to the Missouri James boys. Ancestry.com has Jesse Robert James listed as Ben's 2nd cousin 6 times removed and his father Robert S. James is listed as his 1st cousin 7 times removed.

It is apparent that Robert Sallee James was 1st cousins to Jesse Woodson James and Benjamin Franklin James.

Furthermore, brothers John M. James and John Peace James Sr. also had a younger brother named Jesse James born in 1770 near Rowan, NC.

Both Jesse Robert James from Missouri and Jesse Woodson James from west Tennessee were 2nd cousins and named after their great uncle Jesse James.

This photo of Fr Joseph Alibert for example was taken in China the year 1860 and shows the clarity difference and lack of chemical spotting compared to the the photos from the 1840's and 1850's.

Although many historians and authors have never even heard of this spectacular theory

surrounding the legend of Jesse James it has been considered by many that Jesse W James faked his death and even more that there has also been a limited amount of KGC historians and researchers like

Bob Brewer and Warren Getler that have touched on the multiple Jesse James theory. When Ben called

the Sac Fox tribe which is the home of famous Chief Black Hawk, the tribe indicated that there was

more than one Jesse James and their Jesse James was considered an Indian.

The last Confederate General to surrender to the union was Cherokee Chief Stand Watie and it

is a known fact to some as well that Jesse Woodson James made alliances with the powerful Chief

Sitting Bull years later in the 1870's while his cousin Jesse Robert James had become completely

recognized as an actual Indian with the Sac Fox nation whose ancestral homelands include Northern

Illinois and Southern Wisconsin.

Ben recognized his ability to track things as certainly being a trait that exists naturally in his blood and

also recognized that Bob Brewer had that same old skill passed down from his Cherokee ancestors.

Ben sensed all along that he was related to Jesse James for some reason and Jesse was certainly also

known for being an expert tracker, expert marksman, 33rd degree master mason, Civil War Veteran, and

an expert wilderness survivalist among other things.

Perhaps the most important thing that the "Quest of the Giant J" has accomplished is providing an

understanding of federal mineral rights for the many people who have been kept in the dark by corporate greed and corruption resulting in a major loss of history and actual wealth to their family.

Since the Great Depression of the 1930's many things have taken place that are a direct attack on the

people and their individual right to property and due process of law which is all protected under the

Constitution but unfortunately the state, county, and federal government do not necessarily enforce

those laws if it does not benefit them or especially if they broke the law and violated someones mineral

rights and private property intentionally or not. They are not going to track you down and tell you that

they sold your great uncles mineral property illegally for taxes and by the way you really are the true

owner of a federal mineral patent where gold was discovered by your ancestor.

As several lawyers pointed out this situation is "Huge"! Bob Brewer said that if Ben was right about

the federal laws in the mineral patents then this would certainly change history and obviously for the

better!

One lawyer said the US Attorney would certainly do something because otherwise this would be

equivalent to them stealing Grandma's piano.

The corrupt mega corporations were attempting to get away with the massive theft of the nations

private mineral wealth which is essentially the true "National Treasure". The only thing stopping the

corruption was Ben and his ancestors who had guided him along this amazing journey into the secret society of the KGC and the Knights Templar.

As a matter of fact the corporate corruption had gotten away with the unforgivable disgrace until Ben

Miller had an unscheduled meeting with his family which just so happen to include such individuals as

President/General Andrew Jackson, Judge Andrew Jackson VI, Lt. General Stonewall Jackson, Colonel

Jesse Woodson James, Benjamin Franklin James, Colonel George Washington Jackson,

Jesse Robert James, Sgt Alexander Franklin James, Colonel Jackson C. Jackson,

Sir Richard Jackson, and Chief Victorio aka "Apache Wolf".

Ben refused to accept their answers of why they were trespassing on the Giant J.

Ben felt a big responsibility to the people and to his country even though he didn't volunteer for this

chaotic adventure. Ben tried to think back and remember if maybe he did volunteer but just forgot? The

Quest of the Giant J was much bigger than anyone could imagine. Ben thought about the bloodline of

God and the unwavering devotion that the Knights Templar's have shown in their efforts to protect the

bloodline or was the Holy Grail really just a cup that Jesus used? Ben was leaning towards the

bloodline of God. He had traced the Jackson's back to 1290 A.D. England alongside the Knights

Templar of antiquity and traced the bloodline of Jesus to a Merovingian kingdom around 800 AD.

There appears to be a 500 year gap from the old Merovingian empires to the creation of the current UK system that was mainly politically constructed and designed by King James who spoke 5 languages and

was the only king in history to not need an interpreter. King James was obviously extremely intelligent

and credited with the political creation of the UK which formed out of remnants of the Merovingian

empires that seemed to hold the last possible evidence of a potential existence to a legitimate Jesus

bloodline and King James had personally authorized the Knights Templar's to control the banking

system in London and designated it as a sovereign nation.

Ben wondered if Jesse James relation to the Templars and the political connection to King James was in

anyway connected to that of Jesus or God? Further research of the King James surname Stuart appeared

to not actually be a blood relation to Jesse James but the blood line of Jesus or God may

actually still be a viable theory as the Templars secrets continue to revolve around the treasure which

includes the possibility of the Holy Grail itself. Some scholars have speculated that the Grail interacts

with the treasure as part of God's Will and participation here on earth as it would be in heaven or his

kingdom. The movie the DaVinci code refers to this scenario as actor Tom Hanks tries to protect the

Grail bloodline from the ambush of worthless demon scum.

Stranger things have possibly happened I suppose Ben said to himself as he closed his Giant J

scrapbook that was now the size of a telephone book. If anybody could track something difficult it would certainly be the "Apache Wolf" or Jesse James. Ben thought about the fact that the Comptroller of the US Currency said in his last phone call that his documents and claim to the Fed were an absolutely incredible story. Ben said thank you very much and that he was thinking about publishing a scrapbook that he had compiled called "Quest of the Giant ". Ben spoke to a few local people in the publishing business and one veteran of the industry told Ben that he would never get a book deal unless he was already in the club. The man also said he would never find a literary agent either who is generally needed to even talk with the big publishing houses. He told Ben to just publish his book himself online and forget about getting a literary agent. Ben thanked him for his advice but decided to make some calls and see what he could find out. After a few calls he was able to secure an agent who ironically happened to have worked with Warner Bros and specialized in movies. The agent said he was interested in the Knights Templars and Freemasons after hearing about Ben 's story. The agent Fred Price was also a 32nd and ½ degree master mason himself and asked Ben to join the Freemasons. Fred was the owner of the Fred Price Literary Talent Agency and had worked on over 200 movies in his career with the majority being made by Warner Bros. Ben had previously developed a business relationship with key sources within Warner Bros Music Studios and now Warner Bros Pictures. It was the spiritual Quest of the Giant J that ultimately led Ben directly to God's army otherwise known as the Knight's Templar and thus is why it says on all Federal Reserve notes " In God We

Trust".

The End

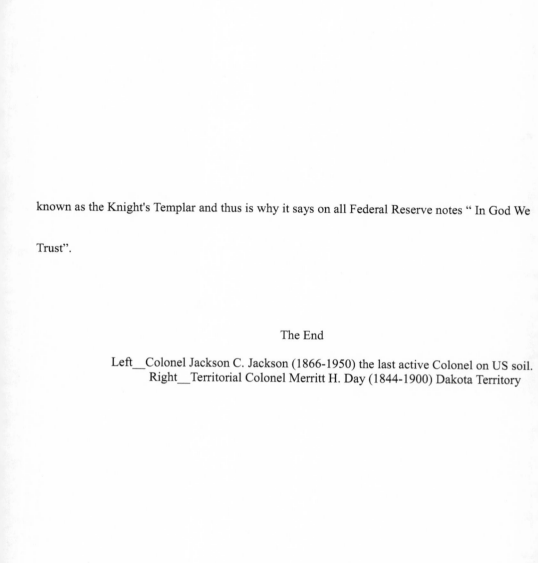

Left__Colonel Jackson C. Jackson (1866-1950) the last active Colonel on US soil.
Right__Territorial Colonel Merritt H. Day (1844-1900) Dakota Territory

References and source material:

-The 2003 Almanac of Record by John W. Wright

-Ancestry.com census and records collections

-General Land Office land patent data base

-"In to The Unknown" Reader's Digest

- "Jesse James Was One of His Names" by author Del Schrader

-"Shadow of the Sentinel" by Bob Brewer and Warren Getler

-South Dakota Historical Society

-Kentucky Historical Society Pence Collection

-Chicago Historical Society

-Chicago Tunnel Story Exploring the railroad "forty feet below" by author Bruce Moffat

-Dickson County Archives in Tennessee

-Various eyewitness and documented affidavits

-Jackson/James family photos, documents, and extensive research provided by author Ben Miller

-Railroads of the Black Hills my Mildred Fielder

Made in the USA
Middletown, DE
14 July 2022

69185626R00144